y t h o l o g y
:the study of youth

J e f f G r e n e l l

We are at the end of what I call The Teen Decade (2013-2019).

It is the seven years of the teens that only happen once each century from 2013-2019.
The past 7 years I have asked God for 1,000 students across America to fast and pray Fridays at lunch.
November 2019 we passed over 1,000 students committed to fast and pray Fridays at lunch.

One of the prayers that I have prayed almost every Friday since 2013 has been,
"God, I promise to bring this generation before you for The Greatest Awakening America has ever seen!"

As a youth leader, we have the responsibility of raising up the next generation of young people in the church to lead the church to its greatest days.
After all, healthy youth leaders create healthy youth ministries.
If the church is in the hands of the youth leaders and the young people that I see across our nation, the church is in great hands.

This book is written for those who want to shape the next generation of young people in the church to reach their world for Christ.
It will look at the history, theology, trends, and future of youth ministry.
As you read this book, would you pray that same prayer that I have prayed since 2013?
"God, I promise to bring this generation before you for The Greatest Awakening America has ever seen!"

OUTLINE

PREFACE

ythology is the study of youth.

Like the study of arachnology. Or the study of miasmology. Or the study of zymology. Kind of. Because to study youth is much more interesting than these. Go ahead and Google those ology's.

Definition of ythology

Let me define the title and the concept of the book. It is the name of my organization, but, it really is life for me. I've shortened youth into the tag *yth*. A popular short for YTH ministry. And placed *ology* at the end of the word because my life-work is to study youth. Here is how it breaks down in language:

> *youth,* **yüth [yooth]** noun. 1. the period between childhood and maturity. *Ology,* **ol·o·gy [ol-uh-jee]** noun. 1. a subject of study; a branch of knowledge. (Merriam-Webster/Dictionary.com)

So, the study of youth. Or, YTH as we will use in the rest of the book.

Really, YTH is difficult to even define. Is it an age? A mindset? Or behavior? It has been defined by some as adolescence (immaturity). It has been defined by others as stages of thinking or behaviors (development). In some cases, it has even been defined by the specific practices or codes in certain cultures or regions by right of passages (societal). One thing is certain, YTH is complicated.

As a working definition for this book, I would define YTH as 'the teenage years of growth between childhood and before adulthood'. And so, I am writing this to help YTH teams in the church, para-church, school, or organizational setting who are working with the middle school, high school, and even university aged YTH. In some organizations this age set is called Next Gen or even Now Gen. We will simply use the term YTH here to include all three sets. I am including university students because about half of the college and university students are still teenagers anyway.

Let's look at a few threads you will see throughout the book. These are the overarching themes or ideas in the book that will be woven in almost every chapter. So to have some understanding of these concepts will make your journey more profitable as you read.

Sustainability

What has excited me about writing this book is the concept of sustainability. The whole idea of sustainability is every organization's focus. There's not a Fortune 500 company on the planet that is not discussing sustainability plans or strategic planning for the future. Executive coaching and life coaches and futurists are a growing consulting emphasis for many organizational leaders as they plan for their future. This concept of sustainability must be a focal point for YTH leaders as well. What are we doing to strategically plan for the future of the church or our organizations? Do we have a sustainability plan?

> *I believe the best organizational sustainability and the most strategic plans an organization can make is to position itself with young people in mind*

One of the key ingredients to sustainability is the big picture - a 30,000 foot view. Understanding the beginnings of, the now of, and the future of an organization or a thing is critical to its longevity and posterity. As it relates to YTH ministry, I think it is important to understand the past, the present, and the future in order to ensure a healthy YTH movement in the church.

The last 36 years I have dedicated my life to *ythology*. I've seen individual YTH grow into revolutionaries and world changers in just a few short years and because of some formative spiritual moments. I have personally seen the impact and the influence of YTH on society – on families, schools, teams, organizations, governments, business, and an entire generation.

In this book you will see the potential impact YTH could have on your setting and on their world. Here's another thread that defines the target we are talking about.

Generational Comparison

With the developing personhood and the sheer numbers of YTH, their influence on society could be noteworthy. In this book we will look at some of the influential young people throughout history and see there are the same influencers living in our present generation. Every generation in human history has seen the impact of young people on every sector of society. Like the prayer of Awakening at the beginning of this book, the future of the church is critically dependent upon its young people.

In order to get a better understanding of the generational comparison, here is a quick data set for each of the existing cohorts. This data is taken from a compilation of demographic research from Barna, Kasasa, and Pew Forum.

Baby Boomers
The Boomer Birth Years: 1944 to 1964
Their Current Age: 55 to 75
Generation Size: 72 Million
Media habits: Baby boomers are the biggest consumers of traditional media like television, radio, magazines, and newspaper. Despite being so traditional, 90% of baby boomers have a Facebook account. The Boomers have begun to adopt more technology in order to stay in touch with family members and reconnect with old friends.
Shaping Events: The optimism of Post-WWII, the cold war, and the Hippie/Jesus People movement.

Gen X
The Gen X Birth Years: 1965 to 1979
Their Current Age: 40 to 54
Other Nicknames: "Latchkey" generation, MTV generation
Generation Size: 76 Million
Media habits: Gen X still reads newspapers, magazines, listens to the radio, and watches TV (about 165 hours worth of TV a month). However, they are also digitally savvy and spend roughly 7 hours a week on Facebook and other platforms.
Shaping Events: End of the cold war, the rise of personal computing, and feeling lost between the two huge generation sets.

Millennials
The Millennial Birth Years: 1980 to 1994

Their Current Age: 25 to 39

Other Nicknames: Gen Y, Gen Me, Gen We, Echo Boomers

Generation Size: 89 Million

Media habits: 95% still watch TV, but Netflix edges out traditional cable as the preferred provider. Cord-cutting in favor of streaming services is the popular choice. This generation is extremely comfortable with mobile devices but 32% still use a computer for purchases. They typically have multiple social media accounts.

Shaping Events: The Great Recession, the technological explosion of the internet and social media, and 9/11.

Gen Z

The Gen Z Birth Years: 1995 to 2019

Their Current Age: 4 to 24

Other Nicknames: iGeneration, Post-millennials, Homeland Generation

Generation Size: Roughly 25% of the population (92+ million)

Media Consumption: The average Gen Z received their first mobile phone at age 10.3 years. Many of them grew up playing with their parents' mobile phones or tablets. They have grown up in a hyper-connected world and the smartphone is their preferred method of communication. On average, they spend 4 hours a day on their mobile device but 9 hours on screens.

Shaping Events: Smartphones, social media, never knowing a country not at war, and seeing the financial struggles of their parents (Gen X) have made them more financially conservative.

Let's take a quick look at the two sets that will comprise most of the background for this book.

Millennials and Gen Z

It is no secret YTH dominate culture in America. And by YTH I mean the Millennial and the Gen Z set. The Millennials are the demographic set that follow the Generation X of the 1960's – 1980. They would watch the second Millennium change on planet earth. Millennials are the older brothers and sisters of the last demographic to be tagged – Generation Z – the present generation of teenagers. Gen Z, as they would be called by their shorter moniker, are the teenagers and adolescents of today. These two sets are what we will call YTH in this book.

Young people in the Millennial and the Gen Z sets are the focal natives in our society and the pop way of life in modern America. Young people are at the center of the top social and cultural issues of the 21st century as we will see in this book. Additionally, they are in the spotlight of every marketing and media company.

As other authors have written in the past few years, YTH are being courted by the "Merchants of Cool", the creators and marketers of pop culture for teenagers. And teens are being used for profit at the highest bid. At some point, we must see them for who they are and not for how they can be used. As YTH leaders we must shape this powerful resource God has entrusted to us and value them as people and not as a commodity.

These young people in the Millennial and Gen Z set are going to define the next era in American life. They will do that as they *redefine* the sexual revolution, or *reimagine* the information and AI (artificial intelligence) arenas, or *redirect* the social media phenomenon, or *recover* the disintegration of, and comeback of, the family, or even *reinvent* how to deal with causes such as anti-human trafficking, bullying, and humanitarian work. Young people in America today are writing another chapter in our history. In world history for that matter.

Demographics

Let's look at the numbers.

The global picture will prove there is a large portion of the world population that are teenagers and young adults. With this fact comes the importance of such a book - to assure there is a sustainability plan for the church. See the current world clock total population by city, and then, we will compare it to YTH in the United Sates.

The latest Census Bureau statistics show the top ten populated countries in the world as of February 2019 are:

| 1. China | 1,389,618,778 | 6. Brazil | 210,301,591 |

2. India	1,311,559,204		7.	Nigeria
3. U.S.	331,883,986		8.	Bangladesh
4. Indonesia	264,935,824		9.	Russia
5. Pakistan	210,797,836		10.	Mexico

Additionally, according to the UN Office of the Secretary-General Envoy to YTH, there are about 1.8 billion YTH in the world ages 10-24. They would make up the largest country in the world today if they lived in one place. Can you imagine that setting? I would move to that country! This is a significant percentage of the world population. Almost one-third.

According to the US Government and the HHS Office of Adolescent Health, there are about 28 million teenagers in the U.S. and more than 42 million between the ages of 10-19. And these numbers are only growing. In this same statistical study, it was reported there are about 16.2 million High School students in the U.S. (1)

> *YTH development and YTH engagement are cross-cutting issues in the 2030 Agenda for Sustainable Development and other internationally agreed frameworks, as well as, a central aspect of Security Council Resolutions 2250 (2015) and 2419 (2018). Each of which acknowledge that young people play an important and positive role in the realization of sustainable development, in the prevention of crises, and in the advancement of peace.* (2)

The UN has often recognized the role of YTH in sustainable development, the prevention of crisis, and the advancement of peace. I believe it is time the church must do so also.

Do you see the importance of such a generational set? Can you understand how important it is to the future of society that we take serious the responsibility before us to raise this generation of young people? Don't just take it from me. But hear it from the United Nations Secretary General and the U.S. Health and Human Services department about the numerous resolutions placing vital program emphasis and importance on YTH development globally and here in our nation.

The Millennials and Gen Z are no more important than any other generation – except they are demonstratively lacking in the religious realm. Something that requires our immediate attention. One thing will be evident throughout the book is the almost unbelievable lack of spiritual awareness among young people in America.

Let's take a look at another of the common threads throughout the book.

Suddenlies

Suddenlies are what I call spiritual interruptions. These could come in different settings and can take different forms.

In the past five years I have watched some of the most moving moments in YTH ministry across our nation. I have watched as students were struck by the nature of God and theology and His presence in large and small crowds across our nation. The messages I've heard and the messages I've spoken have brought thousands of teenagers across our nation to their knees before God.

The moments I've seen and led are etched in my mind in all kinds of settings across this country of ours. The students and leaders reading this know of these moments in conventions, conferences, camps, retreats, services, flagpoles, and other settings.

We need a significant spiritual interruption across our nation in a variety of settings again and again and again. I've been in too many meetings in my life and have seen it all — salvations, baptisms, healings, miracles, gifts of the Spirit, prayer and intercession, passionate worship, and brokenness and silence. But these moments are too far apart and too few in number.

What we need in America is an undeniable interruption from the Holy Spirit upon the global church that fills us for the greatest missionary thrust the world has ever seen — on every continent, in every nation, leaving no region or neighborhood or village or government or school or workplace without a supernatural habitation of God.

We cannot have business as usual anymore in YTH ministry. Because what we have been doing isn't working.

Interruptions in our Meetings

Suddenlies must begin in the church through healthy spiritual leaders who are guiding young people to a transformative relationship with Christ.

At the local church level and in the corporate setting I am watching a lot of YTH communicators with incredible skill, slick prose, and dripped (dressed) from top to bottom. Now, I have no problem with this. Excellence should be customary for Christians. But, hear me. I've seen enough people shine on the platform. And far too often they, or an outfit, or one-liners, have been front and center instead of the message of the gospel. I think too many of us as leaders have spent more time in front of the mirror and in our closet preparing for a message than on our knees in a prayer room preparing for a message.

God doesn't need another hype YTH communicator. I've been in that setting and you have to. The setting where, unless the preacher gets to a crescendo every three minutes or has the right tone and flow, the crowd is bored. I've been in this setting where presentations are so strong but the response is so weak because there was zero emphasis upon the altar or decision time. I've seen communicators come with the prose, but couldn't lead the response of teenagers at an altar for 30 minutes.

Too Many Legends

Humbly understand what I am saying here.

Many of you have heard me say this often. We throw around the word *legend* far too flippantly. Believe me, I understand when it is used in jest or calling out greatness in someone. But, our generation has anointed everyone a legend. Really? For what? A good message? A lot of followers? What we need more of in the Kingdom of God are *servants* and not legends. I'm not trying to be a kill-joy or archaic. I'm not asking you to stop using the term. Just think about it the next time you want to compliment someone.

No, God or this generation does not need another legend or message from a hype man or woman. This generation needs YTH leaders who will model Holy Spirit power that brings transformation through leadership and sevanthood.

We do not need a shallow presentation and response to God that finds this generation exiting the YTH service or the Camp or the Convention after 70 minutes. We need more than a generation hitting the local restaurant, the snack shack, or bar only to post on social media the highlights of the night that have nothing to do with the ministry. We need more than our highlights of a sick pic of the presenter or the band accompanied by lights and fog, and, the perfect selfie with the squad (after the filter and edits).

> I fear in too many settings we are modeling to this generation that our meetings should be just like the concerts and award ceremonies in this world. A parade of self-aggrandizement stuck on the presentation and the presenter and never gets to Jesus. An evening where the people look forward to the after-party more than living the after-life.

When what we really need duplicated over and over again in this generation are scenes of brokenness, repentance, and intercession of teenagers and young people calling out to God for a nation. We need scenes of teenagers praising God wildly and worshiping Him reverently and listening intensely to the Word of God. What we desperately need in this generation are leaders who will bring the power of the Holy Spirit into these settings with the expectation of response in the meeting that changes lives after the meeting.

There was a momentum with Christianity 50 years ago we have lost today. You will see this proven throughout this book. Given the moment we are in right now, we need another suddenly.

Look at the possibility before us.

Screenagers

Another thread in the book is the social media and screen phenomenon. Screenagers are everywhere.

We are living in a time where we have been given maybe the greatest evangelism tool since the printing press. Can you imagine the reach of the gospel aided by the impact of social media and podcasts and blogging? Instant connectivity. The global online connectivity could become the suddenly for the gospel if we could redeem its use. Can you imagine the footprint of the gospel aided by the impact of social media and podcasts and blogging? These have become a powerful influence on young people.

These platforms could become another forum for leaders to impact a generation because of the following statistics:

- Over 95% of teenagers have a phone
- Almost half of teens say they are addicted to their phones and 80% say they text multiple times daily
- According to a 2015 Pew Internet and American Life Project survey, 92% of teens age 13 to 17 go online daily and 71% of teens use more than one social networking site (SNS)
- The average teenager will spend about 9-10 hours daily in front of screens (phone, computer, television)
- Of the Millennial and Gen Z set, 70% of these young people are listening to a podcast or reading a blog every week
- 96% of online American teens watch YouTube videos, 71% are on Instagram every day, and 41% of teens chose Snapchat as their main social media site
- Snapchat and Instagram are the preferred social media use by almost 70% of teens
- Only about 16% of teens have a fake (Finstagram or Fakechat) and most would rather just be honest with their real account
- More than half of teenage social media users say it distracts them from doing homework or paying attention to the people they're with
- 54% of teens say they wish they could spend their time more wisely on the internet

Multiple sources used in comparison from USA Today, Psychology Today, Pew, Statista, Geekwire, Huffington Post, and The Atlantic

Instead of seeing screens and social media as the enemy, why not see screens and social media as an ally?

With the lack of theology in this generation, these platforms give us a great opportunity, not to promote ourselves, but to promote spiritual content – we can introduce the King to the listener anywhere and at any time. What God and this generation need is a leader and communicator who will bring a prophetic word and response into this Millennial and Gen Z set and foster an environment of brokenness and repentance of personal and national sin in whatever format we have a chance to influence.

Code Writers

Another common thread in the book is the idea of code writing.

What makes the Second Millennium and Twenty-first century teenagers important is that they have become the creators and publishers of group think and ultimately are rewriting the generational social code. They are defining how their generation thinks, speaks, acts, looks, and ultimately the legacy they will leave behind to the next generation who will follow them – whatever we call them.

This social code is something every generation has written. It becomes the tribal communication of a set and ultimately an identity that shapes their society. Rest assured, the identity of the Millennial's and Gen Z, and the society they are building, will be the model the next generation will be watching as they grow up.

> *Enter the church. I believe YTH leaders should be the greatest sociologists on the planet. How can we have a successful YTH ministry if we are not in relationship with YTH? How can we have a successful YTH ministry if we do not understand their world? I believe YTH leaders can guide the code-writing of the students in our ministries if we will partner with them and help them turn the secular into the sacred.*

If the church does not become both *relevant* (in setting with) and *relative* (in relationship with) to the Millennial and Gen Z sets, the church will miss an opportunity to shape another generation. Just like we did in the last generation. It is not enough to be in the setting or cultural context of YTH. That is simply having knowledge or currency. We must be in the setting or cultural context of YTH *while at the same time being* in relationship with YTH. I do not want to be only relevant (knowledgeable, informed, and current).

I want to be relative (understanding, connected, and relational). We can have the knowledge of the code. But if we do not have relationship with the code-setters it will not be enough. Whoever reaches the code writers reaches the culture. To be honest, as YTH leaders we are the code setters. What are we handing off to our students to handoff to their peers? They are watching us.

Content and Context

You will also hear these two terms throughout the book. In various uses. To be honest, this would be a great book in itself.

The struggle between content or context-emphasis. The discussion of content and context will always be a struggle of the balance between the two. Some people will die on the hill of ministry and say *'content is king'*. Others will fight the battle on the same hill and say *'context is king'*. Personally, I say they are the wedded king and queen and cannot live without the other. For it would be foolishness to say content is king if we have no audience. And likewise, it would be foolishness to say context is king if we have no message.

The debate is an important one. In the end it is best to have both. Indeed we cannot do ministry unless we have both as the approach. Especially because while the message has not changed, the audience has. There have been authors who *think critically* about the church and slam the church for its use of outdated context in language or judgmental attitudes. There have been some who *think critical* about the church and slam the church for its outdated content in the culture discussion of morality.

Note, there is a big difference between *critical thinking* and *thinking critical*. The latter is like a poison. You can read it on social media or Twitter daily as antagonists generalize the church into a graceless and uninformed organization. Clearly some in social media are fixated on the negative rather than seeing the beauty of the church. It must be a bummer to live that way – like a pessimist.

For those of us who see the church in all forms and settings in our nation, the church is healthier and more intentional than the generalizations of outdated and judgmental.

I see both content and context in YTH ministry today. Much of YTH ministry in the church is leading the way in becoming a player in the world of the Millennial and Gen Z. Let alone becoming an example for the younger brothers and sisters of these sets who are the newly forming generation yet to be named. Of course, we have work to do. But I'm encouraged by the kind of legacy we are leaving them. The condition of the present YTH ministry in the American church is the incubator for the next generation's potential and for their future role in American spiritual history.

> *If the future of the church is in the hands of the young people that I see across our nation, the future of the church is in great hands*

You will read about the importance of both the content and the context of YTH ministry throughout the book.

The Teen Decade

Another thread that has a major role in the book is what I have called *The Teen Decade*. This has been my life focus and continued prayer for the last 7 years. While I have been writing this book for more than ten years, the book really is the culmination of my life work crafted during this strategic time in human history.

It started in late 2012 as we were approaching *The Teen Decade*. It is the years from 2013-2019. You may not have ever heard that term. But God spoke very clearly to me 7 years ago as I was preparing for 2013. He challenged me to my greatest focus upon YTH ministry during the coming *Teen Decade*. He challenged me to believe for the greatest move of the Spirit in my lifetime and specifically in *The Teen Decade*. Because it only happens once in a century and we will only live in one of them if we are lucky. I feel like a mad man because I have prayed hundreds of prayers the last decade for revival and Awakening.

This topic is my default mindset when I wake and when I fall asleep. The first thing on my mind when I get up and the last thing on my mind when I lay down. I have even spent the last seven years asking teenagers to fast and pray on Friday at lunch. My goal was 1,000 teenagers during *The Teen Decade* to commit to fasting and prayer every Friday.

At this moment, during the printing of this book, we have gone over 1,000 students and leaders who have committed to this! I get DM's on a weekly basis with pictures and messages from students at the cafeteria table or in a classroom or somewhere at their school praying and reading the bible together.

The goal was to unleash a unified effort of YTH ministries across the nation to focus on this time in history. As this book is being written I have asked the Lord to take thousands of prayers and over 300 days of fasting the past 7 years and let that be the backdrop for the reader of this book.

You will hear of the urgency of *The Teen Decade* many times reading through this work. Please whisper a prayer each time you see it. That will result in thousands more prayers for this generation to lead *The Third (Next) Great Awakening*.

The Third (Next) Great Awakening

One of the most important threads in the book, is really the crux of why I wrote this book. Aside from most of the book being written to promote healthy YTH ministry in the church, one whole chapter is spent with the specific appeal to YTH and YTH leaders in the church to believe and behave for *The Third (Next) Great Awakening* in America. A call for YTH and YTH leaders to take this blossoming civil and religious revival we are seeing in our country to the next level.

Awakening means to make someone aware or to rouse them from sleep. We mean it in this book as the spiritual Awakening in a generation asleep to the nature of God the creator of mankind. Deep down in the DNA of every person is the DNA of God. It doesn't matter if they recognize that or not. It doesn't matter if they are male or female, Christian or Muslim, Euro, Asian, African, American, Atheist, Baptist, Pentecostal, LGBTQ+, Democrat, Republican, left handed, right handed, tall, short, old, or young. Every person on the planet was created to be in fellowship with God. But if mankind never awakens to their purpose they have moved further away from their design.

The Awakening happens when humankind recognizes that the two most important days of their life are the day they were born, and, the day they realize why.

We must precede an Awakening in the world with a revival in the church. Revival is not what happens in the world or the culture. Awakening is what happens in the world or the culture. I know we have many different pictures of what that looks like. In all honesty, I don't think it is happening. But we are close. Why do I say I do not see awakening happening? Because if it were happening, we wouldn't be able to deny it.

Look around us at the condition of our society. We may have a lot of issues in America – a post-Christian society, the sexual revolution, social media out of control, materialism, and a divided government. But just because things might look bad doesn't mean an Awakening is out of the question. In fact, it almost sets us up for an Awakening. Because I believe God does His greatest work in the midst of our greatest need.

> *What we really need is a revival in the church so undeniable it is not the church publicizing it, but, it is the world looking in awe at what is going on in the church and experiencing their own spiritual Awakening. Revival may impact the local church, but, ultimately if it is revival it will awaken a city, a region, and a nation.*

The Role of YTH in Awakenings

I believe we are moving closer to a civil and religious Awakening of sorts. Civil in the sense that YTH are taking over our society and playing prominent roles in every sector of American life – government, entertainment, sports, music, and business & corporate. Religious in the sense that given the condition of our society and the kind of YTH that I see in the church, we are in the perfect set-up for *The Third (Next) Great Awakening* in America.

Do you see it? We see teenagers on TV. We see teenagers in Washington, in Hollywood, as professional athletes, in the boardroom, on the internet, and leading in the church. Is it their day? Let's hope so. For many reasons. One of those reasons being the long history of influence young people have had on Awakenings and the place they could have on the next one in our world.

As you will see, young people have played a significant role in the history of Awakenings. There is no doubt young people have begun, and have been at the center, of the Awakenings in American history. It seems these Awakenings have always come at the right time. When nothing else could save the day, when nothing else could stem the tide, and when nothing else could bring hope to a society it was a spiritual Awakening that shook our nation from the beginning of its short history.

We are in the same condition as a nation today again - awaiting the next great move of God.

There have been many significant moves of God in our nation's history. The First Great Awakening of the mid-18th century in the early American colonies, the Second Great Awakening of the mid-19th century throughout the Appalachian and Midwestern states, the Azusa Street Revival in Los Angeles at the beginning of the 20th century, or the Jesus Movement of the late 1960's in central California.

There have even been lesser known movements that were regional in impact such as the Charismatic Renewal in the 1980's and the Brownsville Outpouring in 1995 in Florida. You might even include the explosive church planting growth in the 2000's of many young churches across our nation such as Crossroads Church in Cincinnati, Red Rocks Church in Colorado, Elevation Church in North Carolina, Church of the Highlands in Alabama, VOUS Church in Miami, Hillsong NYC, River Valley Church in Minneapolis, or LifePoint Church in Nashville.

The Great Concern

But even with this kind of growth in these few churches, we are not seeing a nation shifting movement like we've seen in past Awakenings. This is the great concern of the church – that the church is so into the world it is having no effect upon it. What is clear in all of this, is the Millennial and Gen Z sets have not seen a significant spiritual movement in the last 25 years or longer. The Millennial and the Gen Z sets have never seen a spiritual Awakening impact the whole of our nation. They have never seen a healthy church with a national voice. And that's not okay.

Action Steps

Finally, the last thread in the book is a practical section meant to get you to apply some of the things that are dealt with in each chapter. This boxed pragmatic section is a series of questions or simple instructions on how to do application of the chapter content into your YTH ministry.

This is why we must look at the history and the future of YTH ministry. To understand the past, the present, and the future of this important generational set will give us a better understanding of how to help the Millennial and the Gen Z into shaping the future of the church. There will be many more themes in the book, but, these overarching themes or ideas will be woven in almost every chapter. So to have some understanding of these concepts will make your journey more profitable as you read.

"The Sunday School class literally harassed their teacher to death.
So, when I took over the class,
I cancelled an important meeting,
and took the whole class to the funeral of the teacher they killed."
-Dietrich Bonhoeffer, on his resolve to lead his new group of teens who were so unruly that they had driven their first teacher to death

Chapter 1

The History of YTH Ministry: The First 100 Years
(Sunday School era through the Student Volunteer Movement circa 1820-1920)

The foundations of anything may be the most important component of its makeup

The beginnings of YTH ministry are actually quite recent and in some ways difficult to chronicle, but, exciting to research. One of the little known YTH leaders of the early 20th century was Dietrich Bonhoeffer. Many have seen him historically as the popular theologian and Nazi activist that he was. But, it is unmistakable that Bonhoeffer had a first love many do not speak much of. This love of YTH and children impacted the beginnings of YTH ministry as much as anything or anyone else.

Bonhoeffer's passion for activism and theology were only surpassed by his love of children and YTH. One of the most revealing of his thoughts is found in this statement, "The ultimate test of the morality of a society is what kind of a world it will leave for its children". Again, Bonhoeffer says of the importance of raising children, "The child learns to speak because the parent speaks to the child. And the child learns the language of the parent. So the parent must speak to God and learn the language of God that they will speak to their children His words." (1)

Wow. Don't miss that. It is a major part of this book.

Set in the middle of about 200 years of YTH ministry history, Bonhoeffer became a fulcrum and an example to many YTH leaders of the importance of youth and children. Not only in the church, but also, in the community. Not necessarily because he elevated YTH above everyone else. But more so because of the imbalance toward the importance of YTH and trying to center that emphasis. As we look at the variety of movements that shaped YTH ministry, keep in mind one of the most important catalysts for our work can be found in the pages of *The Cost of Discipleship*, by Dietrich Bonhoeffer. If you are looking for a supplemental read, it would be a great one.

Let's take a look at a general timeline for YTH ministry.

There are other people, organizations, and movements that have shaped the history of YTH ministry. There would be no way to accomplish an exhaustive review of the history of YTH ministry in a chapter. It would require a whole book. There are a few streams I have chosen not to detail here because of the time and space issue. But, the people and movements in this first chapter are inarguably the early formulators of what we call YTH ministry today.

> If we are going to shape the next season of YTH ministry from where we are today, having a good understanding of the history of YTH ministry is critical. It helps with coming to the 'why' in our work. Hopefully you will agree, there are some things that need very little change – such as the wheel, the pencil, the basic rules of sport, and YTH ministry.

I believe the most influential moments that shaped YTH ministry in the last three centuries are pretty clear. I will try and place them in a timeline of happenings. But, because they bleed into each other quite a bit, forgive the inaccurate overlap in the order. Because so much was happening in a time frame of just the first 150 years from the late 1700's into the mid 1960's, it is almost impossible to create a readable timeline that looks like an accurate continuum of the early era. But we will try.

After looking at the early era influence of YTH ministry, we will then take a look at the last 50+ years of the modern era also. From about 1970 through the present. Let's begin with the early era influence on YTH ministry.

The Sunday School Movement (1820's)

Although Sunday School can be traced back to the 1780's in London, we will focus more on Sunday School in America. The Sunday School movement mostly began in America about the early 1820's. The Church began aged-group emphasis to children and YTH for the training of young people in their Christian faith. Kind of the original 'small group' so prevalent in the modern Church today. But, at the same time in the Church, there was an emphasis upon Church growth and evangelism. And one of the newest ways to do this was to reach the children of the community.

I am using a compilation of articles gathered by students from Indiana Wesleyan University who were doing a Christian Education report for their class. It is a great read with citations and more than adequate academic work. My research found that most sources would agree with the work of these students. Using memoirs, interviews, and a widely accepted now out of print book by Lynn and Wright, these students have left us an exemplary timeline of Sunday School. (2)

Many sources and articles agree Robert Raikes is credited as the early father of the Sunday School concept in England about 1780s. Raikes was trying to keep children off the streets and so opened up a sabbaoth day of teaching for the children of the inner city. This movement swelled across the Atlantic to Philadelphia with the Quakers in 1790, and New York in 1810, and throughout the West in the 1820's before the original states were even added to the union. This movement began so quickly because of the great need of ministry to children. And the organization and structure began quickly.

> In America, the first national Sunday School began in 1824; its stated purpose was to organize, evangelize and civilize. The focus was intentionally evangelical, and so within the next 100 years the Sunday School had become the primary outreach arm of the church. The Sunday School organization quickly expanded to include all ages. Sunday School became a way for unbelievers to be introduced to, and then assimilated into, the life of the church. By the late 1800's, Sunday School was looked to as the main hope for church growth, a view that continued until the mid-twentieth century. (3)

And so this effort called Sunday School began by bringing children into the church from the surrounding communities to teach them life skills, reading and writing, and hygiene care. This became one of the earliest ideas to do outreach and evangelism in the church and it became very effective. So many organizations today do social or welfare or humanitarian programs. But this is not a new idea for the church. Many of the churches in this time would take the Sunday School to the streets on Saturdays to neighborhoods in the surrounding communities.

The graded format of Sunday School evolved into an age-staged program that required many volunteers to be successful. And it was in these early stages of evolution that the small group idea of Sunday School turned into YTH groups we see now all over the country. The leadership of these new YTH groups necessitated a well-trained volunteer who could dedicate their time to a more mobile student than the younger elementary child in Sunday School. And the YTH group ministry began.

Well, maybe not that simple. But it was the formative stages of YTH ministry.

In the book *High Expectations*, author Thom Rainer identified 7 effective methods that contribute the most to effective assimilation in the church. Of these, 3 were directly related to YTH. He noted that the YTH programs, Sunday School, and the children's programs of a church are the most effective methods to close the back door in the church and help YTH and children with the transition into the body of Christ. (4)

There is much more to it than this, but, the concept of Sunday School and the small group evolution is elementary to the development of YTH ministry. This concept of graded and age-staged development is in the DNA and the culture of ministry to YTH. We cannot neglect the historical evidence of graded and age-staged ministry to YTH and children. This part of YTH ministry history is one that cannot be skipped.

Alongside the Sunday School model in the 19th century, we saw another movement grow up at the same time. And this movement would overshadow not just the church and the Sunday School movement, but, it would loom on the horizon of our nation as one of the great culture shapers of our country. Especially with the emphasis upon young people this movement would bring.

The 2nd Great Awakening (1800-1860's)

Here is an interesting thought. That one of the earliest catalysts to YTH ministry would be one of the world's most significant spiritual happenings. We cannot lose the importance of that thought.

Coming off the 1st Great Awakening in the mid to late 1700's was the 2nd Great Awakening in the early- to mid- 1800's. Led by Jonathan Edwards, George Whitefield, Charles Finney, D.L. Moody, and a handful of others, the 2nd Great Awakening shaped not only the church but also society and education in America. From the eastern shores of the United States came a wave of prayer and intercession through preachers who called the church and the nation to repentance. It was about 60 years of fire. When America was lit as we say today. So much has been written on the influence of the 1st and 2nd Great Awakenings on the landscape of our nation. But here is one entry:

> *The Great Awakenings were religious revivals in the British American colonies mainly between about 1720 and 1790's and then into the early to mid-1800's. They were a part of the religious ferment that swept Western Europe in the latter part of the 17th century and early 18th century, and then moved swiftly to American soil. The revival preachers emphasized the 'terrors of the law' to sinners, the unmerited grace of God, and the 'new birth' in Jesus Christ. One of the great figures of the movement was George Whitefield, an Anglican priest who was influenced by John Wesley but was himself a Calvinist. Visiting America in 1739–1740, he preached up and down the colonies to vast crowds in open fields, because no church building would hold the throngs he attracted.*
>
> *In addition to Whitefield, Jonathan Edwards was the great academician and apologist of the Great Awakening. A Congregational pastor at Northampton, Massachusetts, he preached justification by faith alone with remarkable effectiveness. He also attempted to redefine the psychology of religious experience and to help those involved in the revival to discern what were true and false works of the Spirit of God.*
>
> *The Great Awakening stemmed the tide of Enlightenment rationalism among a great many people in the colonies. One of its results was division within denominations, for some members supported the revival and others rejected it. The revival stimulated the growth of several educational institutions, including Princeton, Brown, and Rutgers universities and Dartmouth College. The increase of dissent from the established churches during this period led to a broader toleration of religious diversity, and the democratization of the religious experience fed the fervour that resulted in the American Revolution.*
>
> *The Second Great Awakening that began in New England in the 1790s and extended into the 1860's was generally less emotional than the First Great Awakening but no less impacting. The Second Awakening led to the founding of colleges and*

seminaries and to the organization of mission societies globally. And this is where so many students and young people were introduced to the church." (5)

Without the aid of social media or the information and technology age, it is undeniable that YTH ministry was influenced so greatly by these movements because so many young people were coming into the kingdom of God and the church. The church needed to do something with this growth of the younger population. Do you understand the importance of these early beginnings? Born into the DNA of our work is an Awakening. A revolution of undeniable influence that shaped not only the church, but also, a nation.

Our prayer today is the same, "God, do it again."

About the same time as the 2nd Great Awakening came a strategic movement that would become the missional structure for early YTH ministry. As Sunday Schools, birthed in England, sprang up all over America, there was also a movement of organizations which would do the same.

Para-Church Organizations (1830-1950's)

A growing movement of sister organizations to the church grew up alongside of the church in the cities of America. These para-church organizations were called so because of the term *para* or beside. These organizations came alongside of the church and were led by the popularity of the Y Organization (YMCA and YWCA, 1844). The *Y* stirred the wave of many more para-church organizations that would evolve in the coming years. Organizations like the Gospel Rescue Mission (1831), Boys and Girls Clubs (1860), Salvation Army (1865), and Christian Endeavor (1880).

Following these were many others in the coming years like Youth for Christ, Campus Crusade, Young Life, and Teen Challenge all becoming some of the first social justice-type movements in America into the mid-20th century.

The term social justice can be traced as early as the 1780's by the Jesuit priests and even more common by other social activists up to 1840's. As a modern, continuous tradition, however, it can be identified clearly in Britain from the beginning of the

1780s, out of a diffuse and unstable urban radicalism that had existed. But the work of these para-church organizations like the Y, Gospel Rescue Mission, Boys and Girls Clubs, and the Salvation Army are all credited with the social work and ministry to the YTH on the streets and cities of Europe and America. (6)

Social Justice

What a heritage for YTH ministry. To be conscious of the responsibility of social justice everywhere. I think there is something quite important here. The reality that social justice, as broad as a movement that it is, must begin with the children because they are the heritage of birthing a new paradigm of thinking toward social issues. This is something we cannot lose today in YTH ministry in America. Especially given the key issues and topics trending in America today. Issues and topics such as human-trafficking, bullying/cyber-bullying, mass shootings, and racism must each be a part of the re-education of YTH in our work.

One of the important (and innate) traits within the Millennial and Gen Z sets is their desire for social justice. It is maybe the greatest causal trait of these sets. With this core interest, we as YTH leaders must find our voice in order to help steer this desire into kingdom principles of biblical justice. I believe this will lead to social justice because scripture has always come before culture. We will deal directly with several of the social justice issues throughout the book.

Neutral-site Ministry

One of the strengths the *Y* organizations and other para-ministries modeled to YTH ministry in the church was that relationships could be done in a different setting outside the church. In a neutral setting. This created a public movement of Christianity and young people in the marketplace.

Many organizations followed the *Y* vision and in the mid-1900's, one of the leading para-church organizations that changed YTH ministry was Youth for Christ (YFC) and Young Life (YL). YFC and YL, along with other campus organizations, authored the beginning of campus and community outreach to YTH in their public schools, their social setting, and their homes.

This model would take YTH ministry in the church public and help it to become a player in the secular marketplace.

Every para-ministry has a unique methodology. Here is how *Youth Work Hacks*, a contemporary YTH ministry site defines the YFC and the YL models of para-ministry:

"Youth for Christ led *contextually accessible* rallies for thousands of young people. Young Life, however, focused on individual *relationship-building*. They emphasized 'winning the right to be heard', by which they meant 'gain[ing] the friendship and respect of students before expecting them to listen to the claims of Christ' (Mark Senter, *When God Shows Up*, 2010, p.220). (7)

This was the first instance of *incarnational youth ministry*. What I will often call neutral-site YTH ministry in this book. It was in the 1950s that Young Life first used this kind of term. At the same time of these para-church organizations, another grass-roots movement would take place and become as influential as any YTH movement in American history.

The Student Volunteer Movement (1880's-1890's)

Because of the amount of students and young people who were being born again in the 2nd Great Awakening, there was another movement that broke out right before the turn of the 20th century. It was short-lived as far as the number of years it lasted, but, the influence upon young people was undeniable.

It happened in the 1880's – 1890's and was stirred by the revivals and Awakenings but broke out specifically on the University and the College campus. At its core, the Student Volunteer Movement (SVM) was about going into all the world and making disciples. It was a call upon a generation to "Go..." And it had a verse that became popular in every setting of the movement. *"Then I heard the voice of the Lord saying, 'Whom shall I send? And who will go for us?' And I said, 'Here am I. Send me!'"* (Isaiah 6:8) This would become the clarion call upon a young generation that was given the name the Student Volunteer Movement (SVM).

There were many early figures in this movement, but, none of them more prominent than Robert Wilder and D.L. Moody.

Robert Wilder was a student at Princeton College and the son of missionaries. His father, Royal Wilder, was a missionary to India about 1846-1877. After their missionary work, the family returned to live in Princeton, NJ. Robert was the youngest son and was impacted by the family's missionary calling. And while a teenager, Robert had pledged to go back to India someday as a missionary.

Robert began his studies at Princeton in 1881. In 1883 he and other students attended a missionary conference in Hartford, CT. Inspired by this conference, Robert and his friends went back to Princeton and gathered students and started the Princeton Foreign Missionary Society (PFMS).

Here's a quick review of what happened next.

> "The students wrote a constitution, bylaws, and 40 students signed the charter that included a pledge: 'We the undersigned declare ourselves willing and desirous, God permitting, to go to the un-evangelized portions of the world.' This group would meet Sunday afternoons at Robert's parents' house, where Royal Wilder would share God's word and his own missionary experiences in India." (8)

The missionary fervor spread. Until another meeting took place just a couple of years after this and fueled this early SVM endeavor into a global movement. I believe God can do this again in meetings just like this across our country. We need to get students in proximity of a missionary, of an evangelist, or prophets and apostle's so they can catch the wind and "Go" also. With the global village our teenagers live in we should be dropping a God-sized dream into the heart of every student. They really do believe they can reach the world from where they are because they visit a global village in the palm of their hand every day.

The Mount Hermon One Hundred

The second figure of this SVM was Dwight L. Moody, the most prominent evangelist of the era. When Moody decided to hold an invitation only student conference in the summer of 1886, more than 200 college students from all around the country came to Mount Hermon, Massachusetts. During this month long conference there were many professors and leaders who taught and spoke of the call to missions and taking the Gospel to the ends of the earth.

But, early in this conference something unexpected occurred as the Spirit was moving in Massachusetts.

> "The students would daily gather together with Moody for 6 am prayer meetings, a morning Bible study on the subject of the Second Coming of Christ, and games and sports in the afternoon. Despite Moody's lack of any formal education, he captivated the hearts and minds of some of the best and the brightest college students with a vision of a Great Awakening in the hearts of college students to the revelation and beauty of Jesus." (9)

In the midst of this conference, the young Robert Wilder, now a recent graduate of Princeton, began to envision his fellow students with a dream to evangelize the world in their generation. Wilder spread his passion for a collegiate mission's movement among the other students and the SVM went global. John R. Mott, the future leader of the SVM, remembered, "You could hardly go anywhere without somebody crossing your path and presenting this great missionary message."

It was Dr. James McCosh, then president of Princeton College (now Princeton University), who referred to the SVM in May of 1887 saying,

"Has any such offering of living men and women been presented in this age – in this country – or in any age, or any country, since the days of Pentecost?" (10)

The point of the SVM was that God can use a small number of students to do a great work if they are dedicated to it. The hundreds of students who were released into the world for the Gospel at this time in history was unmatched. Yet, as I watch today's generation, I see the same kind of opportunity. It has happened before and it can happen again. Especially with the characteristic traits of this Millennial and Gen Z set. They are moved by causes and they are moved by campaigns.

We can see the message of the Gospel is attractive. It is viral. It is for the ends of the earth. At the same time we can see the humanitarian or the welfare message of 21st century

Millennials and Gen Z. It has gone viral. It is to the ends of the earth. This relationship seems like the perfect time for an explosion between the Gospel and the causal traits of the Millennials and the Gen Z.

The message of the Gospel that screams "Here am I" is a perfect match for the cause-oriented generation of young people today. But not only for the cause of wells, or for anti-human-trafficking initiatives, or for building sustainable communities alone. But for the cause of the Gospel.

Do you see the influence of these early movements upon YTH ministry today? It is undeniable. With the alarming rate of young people leaving the church after High School and University, learning from the past movements is even more relevant. It is apparent the church must be intentional about calling young people to the cause of missions and a call that is bigger than themselves. The church and YTH ministry must convince our young people of their place in the kingdom of God and the world.

There is too much at stake not to be preaching the missionary message to this generation at this time. If not here, where? If not now, when? If not us, who? Again, this idea of being producers and multipliers is another generational trait within the Millennial and Gen Z sets that simply cannot be missed by the church.

The SVM proved to us when God places His call on the lives of young people and they accept it, they can change the world.

The New Volunteer Movement

While reading an article by Dan Reiland, the leadership guru, I was struck by his comments about how many volunteers there are in organizations. Reiland says, *"There are over 10 million volunteers in only these seven organizations: Special Olympics, Habitat for Humanity, YMCA, American Red Cross, Salvation Army, United Way, and Big Brothers Big Sisters. And there are hundreds of other volunteer organizations."* (11)

As the read this, I was thinking these organizations are not in every neighborhood on the planet. But the church is. The church is the largest volunteer movement on the planet.

It's not the government, or education, or business, or even humanitarian organizations. This reality is that the global leader for organizational volunteers is the church because it exists in almost every community globally. What is for real is that we can thank the Student Volunteers Movement partly for the rise in volunteerism that is so much a part of the global church.

What is undeniable is the church is the largest volunteer movement on the planet. As you consider the impact of the early days of YTH ministry, remember how important the beginnings of something are. These moments and movements undoubtedly shape the most formative years of YTH ministry and must not be forgotten as we forge ahead to our greatest days.

Conversations

Hopefully this will give you some historical background as a YTH leader into what we do and why we do it. Trying to keep the original ingredients of YTH ministry are essential. We will get into this more in the chapter on theology. But, I believe these conversations about the history of YTH ministry would be great discussion with our students.

You can see the importance of beginnings in any movement or organization. Hopefully you have seen the importance of the *moderation of re-invention*. Some things need very little change at the core of their makeup. This is the concept we will detail greater in the chapter on trends. Too often, I think this concept is overlooked in our culture of change. Some people simply change for change sake and not for the need of it.

But as we have said, and hopefully you will agree, there are some things that need very little change – such as the wheel, the pencil, the basic rules of sport, and YTH ministry.

Action Steps

- *How does the beginning of something affect its future?*
- *If Revivals and Awakenings were part of the beginning of YTH ministry, don't you think they will play a major role in the future of YTH ministry?*
- *What is the role of prayer in your YTH ministry? Rate yourself on a scale of 1 to 10 (10 being the best)*
- *Where can you be involved in social and biblical justice in your community?*
- *One of the great ways to promote Awakening and revival is to plan nights of worship and prayer for the YTH*
- *Teach students the history of Awakenings and the importance of revivals. Especially these movements and their influence on the history of YTH ministry.*
- *What would have to change in your setting for the environment to be right for a spiritual Awakening?*
- *Be careful of reinvention excess. And be more mindful of the moderation of re-invention. Maybe what YTH ministry was built upon is much of what we need again today.*

"Jesus is alive and well and living in the radical spiritual fervor
of a growing number of young Americans
who have proclaimed an extraordinary religious revolution in his name.
Their message: the Bible is true, miracles happen,
God really did so love the world that he gave it his only begotten son."
Time Magazine, 1971

Chapter 2

The History of YTH Ministry: The Last 100 Years
(From Billy Graham and The Jesus Movement to The Millennial Era, circa 1920-2020)

The history of YTH ministry is a remarkable journey and understanding its origins will help us to better prepare for its frontiers

As we said in the last chapter, it is difficult to timeline these eras of YTH ministry. As we look at these developing eras, you can tell they overlap. Where one era ended another era was beginning – and this takes place in cycles hard to delineate by dates. However, it is much easier to delineate by nomenclature or movement.

Let's look at the last 100 years or so of YTH ministry.

This is when YTH ministry began to change into the form we have today. There are all kinds of these other earlier elements that still exist today – the graded programming of the Sunday School movement, the Awakening emphasis of the revival movement, the para-church ministry of the *Y* and other organizations, and the interdenominational movement of the Billy Graham era. But, the history of YTH ministry begins to take a turn here. As it develops, it will begin to look very different from the first 100 years.

Of course, there are a plethora of YTH ministry models and approaches nationwide and the models are various in approach. But the emphasis of modernism and post-modernism about to make an impact upon our culture was going to be in the background the next 100 years of YTH ministry history. This next era did not only have an impact on YTH ministry and the church, but, also, on our country. Let's begin with maybe the most influential bridge set in the middle of the 200 years of YTH ministry.

Billy Graham Crusades (1940's-2006)

The next great influence upon YTH ministry in America would become a worldwide impact and last for almost 70 years. It grew up mostly because of a lone iconic person, but, it was driven by the WWII era also. It was at this time the term 'adolescent' was becoming popular because of the number of young people recruited to the war. The discussion in this era was around whether young people could handle a war assignment. I believe the young people of America answered that question as they became a major force socially. This necessitated the church to become a strategic influence in order to capture the adolescent population and their industrious spirit as the war drew to a close.

William Franklin Graham, born in 1918 became unarguably the most prominent evangelist of the 20th and 21st century. His conversion to Christianity took place as a teenager and would be the backdrop for his ultimate influence on the YTH and then general revivals he would lead over the next 50 + years.

Interestingly enough, Billy Graham's own conversion at the age of 17 took place at an evangelistic meeting in 1934 in Charlotte, NC conducted by a young former baseball player named Mordecai Ham. Graham's passion for baseball drew him and Grady Wilson, one of his teenage friends to the meetings held by Ham. There have been countless stories told in many publications, but, here is one account from Mordecai Ham himself on Graham's presence in the meetings.

> *"Two young high school boys attended our meeting. They thought that everything I said was directed their way; so they decided to take seats in the choir, where I couldn't point my finger at them. They didn't pretend to be singers, but they wanted to be behind me. Billy recalled to me later that on first attending the services, he was impressed with the crowd. He had never seen such a crowd, nor such a big preacher. But soon Billy had all he wanted of the meeting. Billy didn't like being told he was lost and going to hell.*
>
> *So he got out as soon as he could and said, 'I am through.' But he was miserable all that night and all the next day and admitted to me, 'I couldn't get there soon enough the next night!' And the next night Billy and his friend Grady both went to the altar."* (1)

The impact of those meetings in Charlotte in 1934 would change the course of many lives the world over. Those meetings would have a major impact on the YTH movement in America also and ultimately worldwide. Because Billy Graham and Grady Wilson would become partners for decades to come and travel the world preaching the gospel and watching thousands of teenagers come to Christ through their work. They would partner with musicians, and athletes, and Hollywood icons to tell generations of teenagers about the saving power of Christ in stadiums and coliseums the world over for more than 60 years. All because of one night in a tent revival in Charlotte, NC about 80 years ago.

Apocalyptic and Eschatological YTH Ministry

We cannot lose the message Graham heard that night at the rally in Charlotte, NC. Did you hear it in the words of the preacher Mordecai Ham? Ham said that Graham didn't want someone telling him he was *"lost and going to hell."*

Follow me here.

Could it be the traits of the former spiritual Revivals and Awakenings could be missing today in our message to YTH?

Could it be we have moved away from the truth of Christ? That we have lost the preaching of hell and heaven and death and eternity? Could it be we have lost the urgency of Apocalyptic and Eschatological preaching to teenagers? That we are afraid to preach the truth of the Gospel because we are afraid of the audience and how they will respond to us?

The problem in our message today is that we haven't convinced people they are not okay. A message pop psychology counters with 'I'm okay, you're okay!" Have we forgotten God's judgment, and not just His mercy, is upon us right where we are at. That we better change or else.

Could it be the traits of the present message for spiritual Revival and Awakening could be what is actually keeping YTH from the message?

Could it be we have moved solely to the message of the grace of Christ alone? That we found the preaching of the here and the now and life without ever talking about eternity. Could it be we have become really good at cultural preaching? That we have become really good at preaching the grace of the Gospel because we are not afraid of God and how He will respond to us.

The problem in our message today is that we have convinced people they are okay and God's love is upon us and there is no need to change. Read those last two paragraphs again. Do you see the difference in the message?

> I know I take the risk of most of my young readers disagreeing with me. If you know me, that is why I am saying it. My young readers will say our generation won't respond to truth. I am pushing back and saying 'really'? I'm not so sure this generation has even heard this message. Maybe your mom and dad did. But not Millennials and Gen Z. We've been stuck in an all grace message for 15 years in YTH ministry, and the larger church for that matter. How is that working for us?

I mean, there used to be plenty of truth in the message of the past. It was those moments in American history that shifted our society. But now there is plenty of grace in our message today and look where that has gotten the church and our society. It has gotten us to a place where the church has lost its message and its authority and our society has gained theirs. Maybe the church today has lost the message, the complete message of God.

The message of both truth and grace.

In the Barna Trends 2018 report, the research purports that "people are turning inward for truth" and "what is right for your life is best for you." Mostly because people are finding it harder to trust spiritual authority and they are instead turning inward for truth. (2)

What an eye-opening finding. That maybe the reason why people are not in agreement of what truth is may be because they do not trust the truth-bearers. It is true that relativity is rampant. But could it be the erosion of truth in society is because of the erosion of trust in the saints?

The problem is not the message. It is the messenger.

I believe broken and weeping messengers could be extremely believable in our society. When I was growing up I had great respect for my spiritual leaders – for most spiritual leaders actually. Pastors and spiritual leaders were revered. But we do not see that today. For many reasons. As Barna said, the main contributing factor is definitely disrespect for authority in ministry. This is why we need a new breed of spiritual leaders to define God to this generation through brokenness. Mankind already knows we have issues – we just need someone to tell us in tears through empathy and compassion and truthfulness.

I can remember being afraid of God. In a healthy way.

Heaven and Hell

When I was growing up, I wondered if the Lord would return by the end of the day or even that night. We were told by the preacher that if there is sin in our life we were separated from God. If I am separated from God and He were to return, I would not spend eternity in heaven with Him. And yet, knowing this did not harm me or make me judgmental or look at God and call Him unjust or angry. That did not make me cynical. It made me aware of a part of God our young people today do not know – the fear of God. The message Billy Graham heard that night in 1934. That God loves us jealously and does not want to leave us where we are.

What a lost message today. How does that even sound to you? Awkward and heretical right? Your defenses come up when you read it over again don't they? Maybe it is the missing piece in the next Awakening we will see in America. Just like the impact of Billy Graham. If our message of grace hasn't worked, how about the fear of God?

I mean it. Every word I just wrote. We have lost the fear of God.

It was this call to repentance and to holiness in the Billy Graham crusades of the mid-20th century that shook a world that heard his message. The same uncompromising message that brought his salvation and life change at the age of 17 – and in the years to come, this would be the reason why Graham sat with every living President in his lifetime. He was respected. But not just for the way he lived or for the person he was. But for the uncompromising message of both Truth and Grace he brought.

Don't get me wrong. I'm not asking for the pendulum to swing to judgment without love. The message of the Gospel is grace *and* truth! To merely live in one and not the other is *our* message and not the *Gospel*. I just think we need to swing the pendulum back and forth and let both exist together. History has spoken. A history that shaped our work as YTH leaders. So I ask you, "What will be the history of preaching we leave for the next generation?"

> The history of YTH ministry was born in the message of the Revivals and the Awakenings of the past. I'm not sure it is good for us to build the future of YTH ministry on any other message.

Jesus was not afraid to speak of heaven and hell. Of life and death. Jesus was not afraid to speak of grace and truth. Of mercy and judgment. His message and His methods were clear. Of course, the method will change but the messenger need only speak with conviction and brokenness. That is critical because of how far away from the whole gospel we have moved, the message of both grace and truth cannot be separated if we seek to impact this generation the way Graham impacted his.

In his letter, *"My Heart Aches for America,"* the 93-year-old Graham wrote that he recalled how his late wife, Ruth, once expressed concerns about the nation's "terrible downward spiral"—exclaiming, "If God doesn't punish America, He'll have to apologize to Sodom and Gomorrah."

Graham later wrote he wondered what Ruth would think of the country today where "self-centered indulgence, pride and a lack of shame over sin are now emblems of the American lifestyle."

What is unfortunately true, is that the message of Truth *and* Grace has been lost somewhere between the early and the modern history of YTH ministry.

Inter-denominational Youth Movements (1950-1982)

It can be easy to get caught up in our own faith circles and run in our own lanes when it comes to influence and history. Research often has its own familiar default and framework. Let me open up this history of YTH ministry to a broader scope. Much of the influence and history of YTH ministry I have shared so far comes from the Methodist and Pentecostal streams. But there is more to this. The Baptist's and the Catholic's have their own YTH ministry influence and beginnings.

Baptist YTH Revivals in Texas

One of those big influences in YTH ministry history for the Baptists would have to include the Texas 'Youth Revivalists' as they are called. Here is a quote from a story in the Baptist Press from 1999. It is addressing the revivals in the South where several student revivalists were traveling from Baylor University and sharing the gospel in youth meetings throughout the South in 1949 and 1950.

> *"God worked a miracle by inspiring the young men from Baylor University to take their message of Christianity around Texas and across the South. The movement had a major impact on Southern Baptists after World War II. The youth movement coincided with a return to revivalism after the war, typified by Billy Graham's early Youth for Christ movement in Chicago. Some of them were barely teenagers. But they were preaching the gospel all over the South.*
>
> *We now look forward to what God may do in the next 20 years and beyond and wonder what kind of nation-shaking revival God may grant us. Regardless of the powerful revivals that God had blessed this nation with, they all seem to fall short from the Awakenings in the USA, Wales, Hebrides, and others from early the 1700's through the early 1900's. Yet we cannot underestimate what God has done recently."*
> (3)

This following quote, written only 20 years ago, was a prophetic review of YTH ministry in the 1950's. Do you see the comprehensive affect these early revivals had on YTH ministry? It is undeniable.

"Many of us had been in World War II and were seeking answers, and so these youth revivals in Texas provided some basics for religious experience", said Dr. Arthur L. Walker, Jr., a retired Samford religion professor. (4)

Walker recalls attending one of those YTH revivals, the 1949 youth-led revival that drew 5,000 people to Birmingham Municipal Auditorium, and the impact upon everyone who attended as they left the meetings and took their new-found fervor with them to cities across the south. No doubt the Awakenings hitting America were wide-sweeping in influence and spreading beyond denominational walls.

Catholic Social Services

These inter-denominational meetings continued for about 30 years with the evangelistic fervor that resulted from the Billy Graham crusades and became a unifying presence across America. The Catholic Social Services was a large organization that would play a vital role in the inner cities of our nation and attempt to bring the gospel to family services.

There were many programs such as catechism, discipleship, mass, and other services such as shelters, counseling, and family assistance. The Catholic Social services are still a humanitarian player in communities across our nation today. The interdenominational Baptist and Catholic efforts were great relationships with me everywhere I was working in the church. I remember sharing my YTH ministry each year with another YTH pastor from a different stream than my Pentecostal background.

All of these movements in the mid-1900's would get another wind from what would take place out West in what would prove to be the most influential spiritual movement in modern American history.

The Jesus Movement (1967-1978)

Time Magazine had these words to say as they covered this historic revolution:

> *"Wanted: Jesus Christ. Alias: the messiah, the son of god, king of kings, lord of lords, prince of peace, etc. Notorious leader of an underground liberation movement, wanted for the following charges: Practicing medicine, winemaking and food distribution without a license. Interfering with businessmen in the temple. Associating with known criminals, radicals, subversives, prostitutes and street people. Claiming to have the authority to make people into God's children. His appearance is typical of the hippie type—long hair, beard, robe, and sandals.*

Jesus is alive and well and living in the radical spiritual fervor of a growing number of young Americans who have proclaimed an extraordinary religious revolution in his name. Their message: the Bible is true, miracles happen, God really did so love the world that he gave it his only begotten son.

Christian coffeehouses have opened in many cities, signaling their faith even in their names: The Way Word in Greenwich Village, the Catacombs in Seattle, I Am in Spokane. A strip joint has been converted to a 'Christian nightclub' in San Antonio. Communal 'Christian houses' are multiplying like loaves and fishes for youngsters hungry for homes, many reaching out to the troubled with round-the-clock telephone hot lines. Bibles abound: whether the cherished, fur-covered King James Version or scruffy, back-pocket paperbacks, they are invariably well-thumbed and often memorized. 'It's like a glacier,' says 'Jesus-Rock' Singer Larry Norman, 24. 'It's growing and there's no stopping it.'"
-June 21, 1971 Time Magazine cover article (4)

In the late 1960's, in San Francisco, California, the Bay area would see an Awakening that stirred the West and ultimately the rest of the country. And to most historians, its affects were known globally also. We call it *The Jesus Movement*. A grass-roots Awakening which started a cultural phenomenon that influenced a wave of young people into the church. With this wave came an increasing need to disciple these young converts. Because of the increasing numbers of young people being born again, many churches and organizations began placing more emphasis upon YTH than ever before.

The Jesus Movement came at the right time.

Sometimes when a nation is at its lowest it is the perfect time for a comeback. That is what happened in The Jesus Movement. In the midst of the racial struggles happening in The Haight neighborhood in San Francisco and other communities around the nation like Memphis and Birmingham, the Jesus Movement started a religious revolution that would alter America.

Reading the stories of previous national revivals and Awakenings, I have seen moments in the U.S. that have approached viral proportions. But nothing like this. I've heard people say things like, "man, our church is experiencing revival." Let's be clear here. We may have had pockets of outpouring, but, there is a much greater need today than simply outpourings in our own church. I don't believe God is as interested in our services as a church community as He is our service to our city. We need another a Jesus Movement magnitude impact.

When America is in another spiritual Awakening it won't merely be about services at our church or in the YTH group. It will result in service to a world in need of Jesus.

A Supernatural Influence

To put it into perspective, The Jesus Movement was radical and it turned a nation upside-down. It seems clear today there are greater religious movements globally than here in America. Just look at the epic growth of the underground church in Asia, the supernatural aspect of the healing revivals in South American nations like Argentina and Brazil, and the legendary attendance of the African crusades under the German evangelist Reinhard Bonnke where millions of people are being born again.

Each of these are drawing tens of millions of believers and seeing reportedly millions of converts and miracles and healings. These movements and The Jesus Movement were and are not about good services. It was about lost people being born again and the supernatural signs and wonders of the kingdom. These movements become viral when they are *super*.

In his book called *The Jesus Movement in America*, Edward Plowman, himself raised in the movement, recalls the beginnings of this nation-shifting phenomenon.

> *"When the first Christian coffeehouse in Haight-Ashbury opened in 1967, street Christian workers did not have to argue for the existence of the supernatural. Most street people already knew the supernatural was a real realm and they were soulish beings somehow related to it. From 1967 on, ever increasing numbers of the lost turned to Christ for the answer. It was their psychedelic drugs that paved the way.*
>
> *Through drugs I discovered that spiritual phenomena I was experiencing was an ever present reality influencing all men. And the meaning and purpose of life that came from Christianity was the perfect setup for a generation of young people who couldn't find it in the drug and hippie culture."* (5)

Our world is familiar with the supernatural, but, the church is foreign to it.

What most American teenagers are completely comfortable with, the church is completely uncomfortable with. In the church, we almost apologize for the move of the Spirit. Because of this, teenagers have lacked a true revival of undeniable affect in their lifetime partly because of a lack of emphasis upon signs and wonders and the supernatural. The Jesus Movement was proof of this. Yet the Jesus Revolution is something teenagers today may have only heard of - if they happen to be church-goers at a church that values our heritage.

History is clear every Awakening of significance in America was begun by young people. It may have been sustained by adults, but they were begun by the young people. The Spirit is no less powerful and real today. But, western Jesus-followers have yet to see an Awakening of epic or viral or supernatural proportions as The Jesus Movement of the 1960's and 70's. Whether because of materialism that causes a lack of dependence upon God, or, post-modernism that has given America a breadth of gods and religions to turn to, or, the paralysis of the church, we haven't seen a significant revival in the lifetime of US teenagers.

Public Gatherings

Marked by music, concerts, outdoor festivals, gatherings, and house meetings, The Jesus Movement took Christianity public like the early days of the Great Awakenings. Coming off the beaches and out of bars were the next great leaders of the church and society. Whether that was Pastor Chuck Smith of the Calvary Chapels nation-wide, musicians like Randy Stonehill and Andre Crouch, or Keith Green, or, government leaders and business owners of Fortune 500 companies, the revolution changed America because it changed the people of America.

It is clear The Jesus Movement took Christianity to the public forum.

The influence was vast on the religious landscape in America. Some of the fastest growing U.S. denominations of our day, like *Calvary Chapels* and the *Vineyard Churches* trace their roots directly back to The Jesus Movement. Many other organizations such as *Jews for Jesus* and even the *Contemporary Christian Music* industry called The Jesus Movement the most significant and lasting influence in their history. So many young people were coming to the message of the Gospel there was no room to put them.

What is also clear is the Jesus Movement fueled the growth of an emerging strand within evangelical Christianity. Much like the masses of young people who were coming to Christ around the Second Great Awakening, it was the Jesus Movement that began to place the focus of their attention on the contemporary YTH culture. Many of the young leaders who were central figures of this movement either began themselves as YTH leaders, or, discipled many of the YTH leaders who would lead the next growing movement that would shift American YTH ministry.

The effects of this historic Jesus Movement would linger as a residue on this next movement.

The Mega-Church Movement (1982-present)

Most of the leaders of the Jesus Movement would end up in some way or another leading the great Mega-churches in our nation over the next 50 years or so as Lead Pastors, YTH Pastors, Executive Pastors, or Worship Leaders. And their influence was noteworthy.

About the time the Millennials were being born, this powerful wave of YTH ministry in the larger church rushed across our nation. It was stirred by a growing number of mega-churches with full-time YTH ministry teams that placed a major emphasis upon the middle school, high school, and university campus. These mega-churches were churches that would have attendance of 1,000 and more. Now today, the description has largely changed to 2,000 in attendance and more and expanded to giga-churches with multiple 10's of thousands.

These mega-churches sprang up about 20 years before the turn of the century, in the 1980's, and the mega-church and their YTH leaders would stir a generation of young people to take their faith to the public schools and transform the way YTH ministry was done in the church at the time.

Personal History

I was born in San Francisco in 1963 just 4 years before the Jesus Movement began in 1967. I remember growing up in junior high in a smaller church and everything being about the YTH service and getting a burden for my friends at school. About 10-15 of us met in a small room in our church in Redwood City, California (a suburb of San Francisco). My formative moments of YTH ministry and adolescence were of skateboarding to see my friends in YTH group and school and watching the 49er's.

That YTH group got me hooked on church even though I really don't remember programming and games being the focus. It was all about God's presence and how different it was from the rest of my world. Did you catch that? How different it was – not how similar it was.

But as I moved into high school to a larger church in Grand Rapids, Michigan, everything changed. Now the YTH group was a sub-culture with a cool YTH pastor, great music, creative arts, inspiring messages, exciting events, and a lot of teenagers. Over the next few years my YTH pastor would show up at my school and my athletic games and would have a huge impact on my faith as I entered college in 1981.

Growing up in High School in this larger church setting would impact my life and give me the tools and the vision to then become a YTH pastor in one of the top 5 mega-churches in our denomination shortly after I graduated college. So I know the DNA of this kind of church and the influence it can have.

Criticisms of the Mega-church

In the early days of the mega-church movement there were criticisms. But don't believe everything you hear if you haven't experienced it.

> *I was in one of these top five fastest growing churches and knew many of the other young leaders in the other mega-churches across the country. Sure, there had to be a level of administration and organization. But that was still second to the presence of the Holy Spirit. We were as concerned about theology as we were strategy. And we spent more time emphasizing presence than programs.*

The criticism ranged from their weakness in discipleship, the message of the gospel was watered-down, and it was all about numbers and programming. There were arguments that the setting was too organized and polished. That all mega-churches taught a materialistic gospel and were led by pastors who lived in big houses, had flashy cars, flew around the country in private jets, and had affairs with their secretary. Sure, some of these things were happening at this time, but, these were the major minority and certainly not my experience or the experience of many of my friends who were also leaders in some of these large churches.

I've always felt these generalist statements were unfounded descriptions of the overall mega-church.

Because of the nature of this book, this section is not about the general weakness or strength of the mega-church. I am going to stay focused upon the influence of the mega-church YTH ministry. These churches actually looked a lot like The Jesus Movement again as a presence-based model of YTH ministry swept our nation from one coast to the other.

In my experience, seasonal outreaches, camps, conventions, and campus access were all part of the structure of these YTH departments. One of the foci of myself and other friends of mine in these mega-churches was our involvement with other local YTH groups and most of the para-church ministries in our city. We realized it would take a team to reach the thousands of students in our public schools.

Isolation and Culture-building

It can be at easy to become isolated as a large church YTH pastor. It can be easy to pull away from other organizations and even your denominational programming and to build your own brand and culture. I know this is popular today with many large churches. Believe me, I get it. We experienced that kind of growth and development in our YTH ministry 30 years ago and we were running the numbers and had the resources to become autonomous. But we did not.

> *When it would have been easy to do our own thing as a large church and separate our YTH culture from the rest, we decided to make an effort to contribute to the missions giving of our denomination, to attend Camp, bring busses to YTH*

Convention, and impact other local YTH ministries within our state. We were going to raise the level of the other ships in our harbor. We were not having a parade in our city to show off our brand.

I decided to be a team player and to remain in a cooperative fellowship with the other YTH leaders in our area and region because it would be easier to reach our target together. Trust me. I understand the thinking of large churches today – they can do it better, they have the resources, they can bring in global speakers and bands, and they don't have the time to go to area meetings. I refused that thinking 33 years ago. Today I challenge my friends in these large churches to do the same and to ask God how they can influence YTH ministry in their region with a servant mentality like this:

Are you willing to share the wealth of musicians you have, or send YTH leaders or key YTH to a church for a period of time to help their growth? Have you made conferences available to local YTH leaders when you are able? What about inviting smaller churches to your team leadership meetings or YTH services or YTH events?

We are kingdom right?

Traits of Mega-Churches

According to The Washington Post, in a February 2018 article, here are some of the characteristic traits of ministry in these mega-churches:

1. It takes a lot of organization and administration to pull off a weekend of services or a YTH event for a few hundred teenagers
2. Because of the kind of effort it takes to lead at that level, the leaders were a mix of charisma and corporate competencies, as well as, anointed and able spiritual and inspirational leaders
3. These churches had community capital and were often quite involved in the social setting where they were located
4. There were generally a lot of resources available in the mega-church and this allowed for a variety of programs both internally and externally

5. The nation took notice of these congregations of thousands that were impacting their cities with the gospel. Many of them involved in government, education, and the community sectors.
6. Finally, these larger churches had multiple staff – including YTH leaders who were specialized at daycare, pre-school, children's ministry, YTH ministry, and university or young adult programming. (5)

One of the key influences of YTH ministry in these mega-churches was the emphasis upon the school campus and building the relationship of the church and the school. Because YTH leaders in the mega-church were full-time they were able to have a presence and be involved more fully in the public school setting. This is not the same kind of vision today in many of our large churches.

Far too often I speak with large church YTH leaders who are not on campus. Whether that looked like campus access or attending sports and extra-curricular events, or building an emphasis in their students of reaching the public school as campus missionaries, the campus became a focal point of the larger church 35 years ago.

This was never more realized than the most prominent movement that would spring up as this large church movement was developing. *See You At The Pole* (SYATP) would become one of the most important student movements of the 21st century.

See You At The Pole (1990-present)

In 1962-1964 an initiative was launched, but certainly not the sole promoter, by Madalyn Murray O'Hair to remove mandatory Bible reading from our public schools. In addition, it was also the Engel V. Vitale Supreme Court ruling that removed official state-sponsored prayer. (6)

Of course, no one wants a mandatory religious prayer or reading. We would never be able to settle on that form anyway. One thing that was not accounted for in this initiative many years ago, however, was that you cannot remove praying students and Bible reading students from our public schools. This is no different today. Because coming to a campus near you was one of the modern day Awakenings that would leave its mark on America in a significant way.

It really began about 30 years ago in a public school outside of Dallas, TX.

> *Organized by a young middle school girl and her youth group in the Dallas/Fort Worth area, the annual prayer meeting called See You At The Pole (SYATP), has been one of the largest prayer meetings in the history of the world. More than 7 million students will pray world-wide every Fall around the flag poles of their schools. And about 4.5 million will pray every Fall around their flag poles in America. That cannot be legislated.*

I believe this generation of campus missionaries is going to lead *The Third (Next) Great Awakening* in America from the school campus and become another grassroots movement shaping the history of YTH ministry. In 1962-1964 prayer and bible reading may have been legislated from our public schools, but, they were not removed from our public schools. Because as long as our students are in the public school, there will always be prayer and bible reading. You cannot legislate religion in or out of our schools because there are so many campus missionaries (students) who have taken their faith public.

This SYATP movement has placed an important focus upon YTH ministry in the public school setting helping students to take their faith to a neutral site outside of the Church. We must not allow those who have initiated the discussion of ultimately taking prayer out of schools to succeed. Our involvement with SYATP is the proof of this because there are moments in everyone's life that require commitment. I believe SYATP is just such a moment for this generation – will I or won't I go public with my faith?

I have never missed a SYATP since the inception 30 years ago. Sometimes alone, sometimes in the rain, or snow, or even in a plane flying over a county of schools, but, mostly with students and leaders who have something to say about the place of Christianity in America. You cannot write the history of YTH ministry without including this global movement. A movement which began in the heart of a teenager and has spread to an entire generation for three decades.

It is my goal to be at every SYATP in my lifetime so students can see the importance of this movement in my life.

What I would like to see moving forward is for YTH ministry to make a renewed commitment to SYATP. To put our creativity back into this movement and not lose the impact of prayer on the campus. The history of this movement is set in the fabric of YTH ministry. Could we move it to the campus weekly? Or monthly? Could we have all of the para-church organizations meet at the pole weekly or monthly? What if we emphasized this as not just an annual event but a regular movement? If an idea was good for 30 years, why can it not be good for 30 more years if the Lord tarries?

What this movement did was re-birth the para-church organizations and blow the wind back into their sails. Buoyed by an army of campus missionaries, there were bible clubs and prayer groups meeting in public schools across the nation. It was as if the 1962-1964 efforts of Madalyn Murray O'Hair were never felt because of the national emphasis of YTH ministry on the school campus.

This mega-church and para-church movement gave way to the next powerful influence in YTH ministry in America. The era we are in today.

The Millennial Age of YTH Ministry (2000-2020)

This present era we are in is a unique time in American YTH ministry.

What we see in the U.S. really does look much like a compilation of every other era. Depending upon your approach and the kind or type of church you are in, this modern era of YTH ministry will range from production, programming, presentation, and sometimes even presence-based models of ministry.

I will use the term *Millennial Age* of YTH ministry as the general term for the last 20 years. But within this Millennial Age of YTH ministry is a unique characteristic that has grown up and become dominant on the landscape YTH ministry in America. I call it the *Industry trait* of YTH ministry.

Let's look at the Merriam-Webster definition of this word and how I am using it for this next era in YTH ministry:

industry |
1 a: manufacturing activity as a whole (the nation's *industry*). **b:** a distinct group of productive or profit-making enterprises (the banking *industry*). **c:** a department or branch of a craft, art, business, or manufacturing. **d:** systematic labor especially for some useful purpose or the creation of something of value.
2: diligence in an employment or pursuit or habitual effort
3: work devoted to the study of a particular subject or author (the Shakespeare *industry*)

Put all of these *industry* definitions together and you get something like this:

"The activity or production of a specific department or branch in the church, with a useful purpose that creates value through diligence and habitual efforts toward programming for specific ministry to adolescents or teenagers."

When you look at that definition you can see a picture of YTH ministry today. Gen Z are producers and publishers. They have a voice – and for them it is easy because of the many platforms available to announce their footprint on the world. Whether it is a poem, a photo, a TikTok video, or other social media format, YTH today have an instant publishing tool in the palm of their hand. This viral footprint is not going away.

But, what has happened is that this present age of YTH ministry has been influenced by production, activity, compartmentalization, specialization, and social branding. This is evidenced by the hiring of YTH leaders, training of teams, resourcing of next generation departments, unique names for the YTH group, slick YTH events, the growing numbers of National YTH Conventions, and the sale of YTH merch and brand through social media. None of this is negative. It is simply an emphasis of the industry in YTH ministry.

Let me give you what I see as some of the characteristic trending traits (not meant to be positive or negative) in the modern Millennial or *industry*-type YTH ministry:

- A modern Millennial YTH ministry has a unique name, culture, and identity separate from the church. Although there is a growing movement of YTH groups that have adopted the whole church name into the YTH ID, not everyone has made this move.

- Today's Millennial YTH ministry is heavily built on production and entertainment and programming as the method of operation - even the small church setting is influenced by this emphasis. That can be seen in the efforts of creating attractional ministry to students.
- Most of the Millennial YTH service settings include program-based service with mood A/V staging, music and worship, announcements, offering, either an organized and exciting game (or, an agonizing and boring game), a message, and small groups planned within a 75-90 minute time-frame. There is very little presence-based ministry and time for response being practiced.
- A majority of YTH ministries lean mostly to a weekly large group rally mentality and format. But there is also a similar lean to small group time within the YTH service setting and often on a weekly or monthly basis outside of the church.
- Depending on the setting, Millennial YTH ministry is sometimes divided into age-stage and graded junior and senior high spaces similar to the public school
- The Millennial YTH group will often take younger junior high teens out of the Sunday main church service setting and have their own YTH service or experience
- There has been a loss of evangelism and outreach (or *going*) in the Millennial YTH group, and, an emphasis upon inward (or *gathering*) together
- The average Millennial YTH ministry is built around the church campus and getting students to "come" to church rather than emphasizing neutral site events and "being" the church. This has created a codependency in YTH ministry.
- The high majority of YTH leaders – overwhelmingly a volunteer – are more focused upon the attendance at YTH group, rather than the roster or the teenage population on the school campus and the community
- More time is spent organizing a YTH service and planning a message series or preparing for small groups than anything else in the weekly administration
- This present YTH ministry is strongly influenced by social media, image projection, marketing or bannering, and the gathering mentality

Of course, these are generalizations of the definition of the Millennial Age YTH setting but most settings will more or less exhibit these traits. Again, these are not listed to be negative or positive. That will depend upon the philosophical emphasis and approach of each YTH leader. This list is simply observational in my travels.

What is clear to me is a huge need for a return to presence-based responsive YTH ministry.

We will define this term later, but, let me place some ideal characteristic traits for a presence-based YTH ministry so you can see them compared to this millennial age description on the same page. We will get into detail later in the book.

Creating a culture that is presence-based and responsive looks something like the following:

- Pre-event relational capital with students and leaders
- Greater emphasis on musical and fine arts worship experience
- Time spent in prayer and ministry to students
- We need a greater emphasis of the spiritual gifts in the YTH setting
- We need a returned emphasis toward preaching again to create discipleship
- YTH ministry must become more outreach and evangelism focused
- A neutral site emphasis could create more community context-focused YTH ministry
- It is critical to faith development for YTH to have combined worship settings with different age-stage groups
- Monthly, or regular, events that create relational capital in YTH ministry is a must

There will be more said on this in the trends chapter.

Leadership Development in the Millennial Age YTH Ministry

YTH ministry leadership development is a hit and miss commitment in YTH ministry today. Too many excuses about time and commitments and involvements make having regular training sessions together rare.

Here is an overview of Millennial YTH ministry leadership:

First, many YTH leadership teams today have no regularly scheduled meeting at all. There will be a weekly or *weakly* leadership meeting before the YTH service that becomes a pre-service meeting discussing the flow of the evening. But this is not the best setting for comprehensive leadership development.

Second, in a few settings I see a heavily promoted regular leadership development approach through large team-based meetings with the YTH leadership team in the church. This will often be the adult leaders, but, with periodic inclusion of student leaders if they have them too. These are often irregular in cycle – but may happen monthly, or quarterly.

Third, I see mostly individual leadership type emphases in most settings between the YTH leader and a smaller set of volunteers. This is not exhaustive or does it have a comprehensive plan. This is much more organic and under-organized and may happen in a coffee shop somewhere rather than the team based approach.

Fourth, there is a broad appeal toward the external (or internal in the larger mega-church) regional or national conferences that focus on presentation and inspiration. These are usually focused on the large group meeting and tend toward inspiration with guest speakers and bands who focus more upon the quick-twitch spiritual life and not training.

Overall, I have noticed sporadic YTH leadership development in most modern YTH ministries today. Certainly there is very little emphasis on regularly scheduled YTH team development elements such as – strategic training, vision, unity, equipping leaders with generational trait approaches, critical thinking or problem-solving, or even group intercessory prayer for the YTH. Because of the high reality of volunteer leadership in the YTH groups across our country, there is little leadership training in most settings.

> *We must increase the leadership development of both the individual YTH leader and the team. In the larger church setting it is more common to see this leadership development. Although still not very organized or intentional, there is at least cycled emphasis for developing leaders on a weekly, monthly, or quarterly basis. What is clear are the undeniable increased outcomes from intentional leadership development – prayer, unity, clarity, health, exponential ministry to students, culture creation, and ensuing growth in the organization.*

Developing the leadership team may be one of the greatest needs for the Millennial YTH ministry era. We are going to have to be careful YTH ministry does not become solely event and presentation-based in the coming years. Because if this happens, we will fail at preparing YTH ministry and teenagers in the church today with the critical need for exhaustive theological, apologetic, and ecclesiological frameworks.

If someone came from outer-space and visited the average YTH group in America, they would see these kind of things.

In my 36 years of YTH work this is as clear a description of modern Millennial YTH ministry as I can give. Sure, it is anecdotal and general and not scientific. At least in the data mining and research sense. But, it comes from extensive travel in small, medium, and large churches. And it is based upon the urban, suburban, and rural church model in every corner of America. Of course, this is not an exhaustive list of characteristic traits, but, it is general and accurate.

I know you will read this review and agree with some of these things, or, you will read this list and disagree with some of these things. Some settings will exhibit a few of these and others will exhibit more of these. It all depends on the approach and methodology of each leader. Remember, this is a generalization and doesn't apply to every setting. But, what can you learn personally from this review?

Global Educational Emphasis

This bright light on the YTH ministry scene has been a reason for the education of YTH leaders since the 90's. *The educational* movement of the Millennial age of YTH ministry took place in the early to mid-2000's and has lasted strongly into YTH culture today in the church.

It was brought about by brand new thinkers who brought more of a sociological and an educational and academic thrust to YTH ministry. Many of the Next Gen Departments of the Assemblies of God Universities have been training and placing YTH leaders in the local church or para-church settings consistently for many decades. This would include North Central University and the Center for Youth and Leadership (CYL), Valley Forge University, Southeastern University, and Southwestern University.

Other notable academics include Josh McDowell, Chap Clark, Andrew Root, Kendra Creasy-Dean, Pamela Erwin, and, the Download Youth Ministry Podcasts (DYM) of YTH ministry vets Doug Fields, Josh Griffin, and Katie Edwards. Include also long time YTH ministry educators like Anthony Campolo and the Eastern University faculty, and, the Fuller Youth Institute faculty of Kara Powell and Stephen Argue have been shaping YTH ministry thought for 30 years.

These educational thinkers have been forming YTH ministry as we see it today in the evangelical denominations across the country and have brought excellence in thought, scholarship, writing, programming, and resourcing YTH ministry for the past 20-30 years. This educational and social emphasis has fueled YTH ministry at the local church and the University level. As youthworkshack.com has said about many of these leading professionals,

> "The missional perspective of the church as a whole started to shift its focus to 'the missing generation' of 20's and 30's. This was arguably the generation failed by the last decades of youth ministry. Because of this, key incarnational authors started to branch out, and – especially in the case of Root – began writing to the wider church, rather than simply youth workers." (7)

Many of these authors have appealed to the church for the importance of YTH as the present church and not just a department within the church. Much of this was the influence of Bonhoeffer and his theology of discipleship of YTH as a critical, but not too critical, part of the church. It was Bonhoeffer's regular interaction of YTH and children and the way he saw adolescence as no more important, but, no less important than the rest of the church. A truly needed emphasis in YTH ministry at this critical time of church growth, resources, egos, and the social growth of YTH in society.

The educational equipping of YTH leaders is critical to healthy YTH ministry. The role each of these plays is instrumental in growing the impact of YTH ministry globally. There is no denial of the increased effectiveness that comes from training. Hopefully we will see a continued emphasis of YTH ministry training and education and coaching that will continue to set an ascending course for YTH ministry into the next 75 years if we have it.

With the growing emphasis of YTH ministry in this educational era, came another smaller movement within the Millennial Age of YTH ministry that cannot be left out. As YTH ministry was growing, it would become more and more important for YTH leaders to be trained. This led to the next Millennial or Industry-age influencer that became a grass-roots credentialing service for YTH leaders.

School of Ministry (SOM)

One of the societal problems that arose in education in the 2000s through 2020, was the cost of education. This actually drove another movement within the church which affected YTH ministry in an indirect way. With the rising costs of education came hundreds of School of Ministry (SOM) locations around the country. The college education in America became too expensive and the local church and many Christian Universities began to offer education and credentialing and leadership degrees in the church setting or online.

To solve this financial crisis in education, institutions created what are typically called the School of Ministry (SOM) or online campus cohorts. This format has been adopted in many University or denominational or district or network levels and offer extensive credentialing and theological and practical education either online or at their home site. Given the high number of volunteers in the local church, these SOM's have become a great setting for the preparation of YTH leaders who may not ever be able to attend University or College.

These institutes or cohorts offer a locally-based education for a non-traditional student. These are often lower-cost options that do not mandate resident status and may only meet a few times weekly for the credentialing requirements. Some of them, which are actually growing in numbers, offer both the credentialing track and an accredited track of under-grad courses that can be taken online and then transferred to a school of choice.

Another trait of these institutes or cohorts is a close relationship with a University or College that will have guided interaction with the programming and the students. These settings are growing in numbers regionally across America and will continue to play a vital role in the development of YTH leadership and ministry preparation. Especially because of the Millennial and Gen Z trait of competitive achievement.

> *In many school districts across the nation YTH groups have seen a decline in the attendance at weekly YTH services because of students who are hustling to get the grades so they are in a better position for a scholarship to University or College.*

With this competitive trait and rising college costs, YTH ministry attendance issues will continue to be influenced by families who emphasize grades for their children. This will also be a challenge to all YTH leaders to extend their own education and training so the church does not under-challenge teenagers and lose them because YTH ministry is not stimulating enough mentally. We will deal with this thought in a later chapter on theology and YTH ministry.

Another influence in the Millennial Age of YTH ministry is the global influence of the worship arts movement.

The Worship Arts Movement

This movement in the Millennial Age of YTH ministry is a stunning one. It is undeniably one of the most influential YTH movements in the history of YTH ministry. In their May 2019 article, youhworkshack.com goes on to comment on this other global movement in YTH ministry,

> *"The popularity of the music festivals of the 90's continued into the 2000's and became increasingly blended with an aim to reach young people while engaging with youth culture more specifically. This development has been influenced by modern recording-house based project churches such as Hillsong, Bethel and Jesus Culture."* (8)

I would add to this present influence the Planetshakers, Elevation Church, and the Youth America contribution to YTH ministry influence. We cannot underestimate this worship arts movement and its impact upon YTH globally. As a matter of fact, this present and the future YTH ministry culture has been influenced by global worship for some time now.

However, what is very clear is the YTH fine arts and worship movement probably began with the euro-pop group Delirious, and, the American pop group Sonicflood and Jeff Deyo at the forefront of this movement. Delirious and Sonicflood certainly led the way for a new sound and a distinct focus of worship and not solely performance. These two movements would force the change that would be led by upcoming movements such as Hillsong (Australia), Bethel, Jesus Culture and many of these other influencers to capitalize on the love of the arts borne into the DNA of Millennials and Gen Z.

It is undeniable that today in YTH ministry worship and fine arts are the central vibe birthed into YTH ministry all across America. With the smartphone accessibility of social media platforms like music apps, Instagram, Twitter, Facebook, and YouTube, teenagers have instant access to these powerful influencers. Including their music and lyric sheets, videos, and other resources such as merch and the many leadership conferences and the culture of these producers.

The sound coming from these early worship movements captured the heart of young people in the 90's and early 00's and continues in the new millennium also.

Finally

What is clear through this past 100 years of YTH ministry is that diversity has shaped what we see as YTH ministry today. The various players and movements in the timeline of YTH ministry are broad. But what is undeniable is that whatever the future of YTH ministry holds, as YTH leaders today in the church or para-church organizations, we have a choice on what we want YTH ministry to look like in the coming years.

Will we use the formative moments of the first 100 years in YTH ministry as our model? Will we use the formative moments of the last 100 years in YTH ministry as our model? Could we use a compilation of the first two eras? Or, will we forge a new way of thinking in YTH ministry for the generations to come?

Action Steps

Asking the following questions will help you to determine if your present YTH setting looks more like the Millennial age traits of the last 50 years, or, looks more like the original DNA of YTH ministry from the first 150 years.

- *What Kind of YTH ministry are you leading? Looking at our description, is it program-based or presence-based? It is program based if you spend more time on giveaways and games and presentation. It is presence-based if you spend more time on worship and prayer and presence in ministry to students. This question is all about the time and prep that you place into YTH ministry weekly. And the measurement or assessment of your outcomes and wins.*
- *Do you have a regularly scheduled leadership development meeting with your volunteers? How often do you have this? Try holding a spontaneous one-day training session.*
- *Is there a model or church that you are watching and learning from in YTH ministry? It is important to help you learn from a healthy example of someone else who is doing it the way you may be leaning.*
- *What are some of the things you can do to break the compartmentalism or isolation that sets in and separates a YTH ministry from the whole church?*
- *Have you built relationships with other YTH leaders in your area? That is an important task of a Millennial YTH ministry and will help you reach the teenagers in your city much faster.*
- *Try to offer pop-up nights of discipleship or worship for students who cannot make the regularly scheduled YTH ministry - or even an off night YTH service on a regular basis to promo YTH ministry to those who cannot make the regularly scheduled meetings*
- *Have you experimented with app-based music playlists for your worship?*
- *Do you value the call to ministry in your students in either the office (of ministry or the field?*

"We are told by a delightful 'expert' that we ought not
really teach our children about God
lest we rob them of the opportunity
of making their own discovery of God,
and lest we corrupt their young minds by our own superstitions.
If we continue along these lines,
the day will come when some 'expert'
will advise us not to teach our children
the English language lest we rob them
of the opportunity of making their own discovery of the language.
This is absurdity."
-Reinhold Niebuhr, American preacher, activist, theologian

Chapter 3

A Theology of YTH Ministry

Teenagers are under-challenged by the church.

I hear this from teenagers on a regular basis. If we are honest as YTH leaders, there is a greater expectation of teenagers in so many other settings as compared to the church. For instance, the school system has a greater expectation for middle school students than we have for them in the church. It's almost as if the church is treating young people 2-3 grades younger than they really are.

The expectations of students at the junior high and high school level is quite high and has shed light on the lack of expectations the church has for teenagers. Have you seen their homework? Do you realize they are expected to be on time, work in study groups, bring their books to class, turn in completed homework assignments, and respect each other in class? The material they handle in school is much more academic than the sermonette's from our weekly series or the small group discussions we might be having in YTH ministry with them.

Ask yourself a few questions. Are we doing the same in YTH ministry? Are we starting on time? Do we expect our students to come to YTH group with their Bibles? Is our YTH ministry content challenging students to think about theology? Are we building a culture of respect and honor? Our role is not entertainment or nannying. Our role is discipleship.

Keep in mind the one thing the church has to offer our students and the one thing that sets us apart from the public schools is a theology of God. This is the one thing we must be excellent at.

This chapter will deal with theology in two sections. We will look at a theology *of* YTH ministry (and why it is important). And we will look at a theology *in* YTH ministry (and how to increase its importance).

Let's deal with the first one at the outset.

A Theology *of* YTH Ministry

I have had a fascination of Dietrich Bonhoeffer and his writings and his life for many years. In December of 2018, while writing this book, I was able to visit Berlin, Germany and spend some time at both the Zionskirche Church where Dietrich Bonhoeffer was the YTH worker and pastor, and, the home where he spent his teen years. This was a highlight of my life. To be able to speak with the present pastor of Zionskirche and to tour Bonhoeffer's home with a historian added so much more to my interest in Bonhoeffer and his YTH ministry.

I took something away from that day from all of the information given to me in a couple of hours of tour.

BonHoeffer as Youth Worker

I know most people recognize Bonhoeffer and his work as theologian and activist. And it is true his death was a direct result of his activism against the Nazi regime. But there is something few people know about Bonhoeffer – that he was actually most passionate about young people than anything else. YTH ministry is what really made him come alive. One of the things he said about teaching theology to students was very profound. It was on one of the walls in the church and it was written in his classic *Cost of Discipleship*. Talking about the difference between ideology and theology, Bonhoeffer urged everyone of the importance of teaching theology to the YTH:

> *"Because Christ exists, He must be followed. An idea of Christ does not require following or discipleship. Christ is not simply an idea, He is a person. And a Christianity without following or discipleship is a Christianity without Christ."*
> (1)

This is the difference between what I like to call *meology* and theology. Meology is simply an ideology or a Christ-less religion. It is a person's concepts and rules without the person of Christ. It is Twitter today with many voices making personal opinionated statements that are not from a theological perspective, but rather, from a meological one - a person's personal theories about Christianity and not the personal idyllic in scripture. A person speaking about the theology of God who doesn't read or study the scriptures. Far too many people today have a spiritual opinion without a spiritual experience.

It is the writing of Bonhoeffer that drives the YTH leader back to a theological culture to the person of Christ in Christianity. If we are willing to be real with ourselves, YTH ministry has failed at this too often. YTH ministry in America has spent too much time in the culture and not enough time in the scripture, and thus, creating a meological subculture within Christianity.

That December trip to Berlin reinforced in me the critical responsibility of YTH leaders to build our work on the scriptures and not merely upon culture. I encourage you to read as much of Bonhoeffer as you can as a YTH leader. It will help you develop a theology of ministry.

Developing a theology of YTH ministry

YTH ministry must begin with theology. To take theology out of YTH ministry is to take God out of YTH ministry. Developing a theology of ministry is foundational to this book. Because YTH ministry is an extension of the church and its mission – that is, to make disciples of Jesus Christ. You cannot make disciples without an emphasis upon the Bible and theology. To take theology out of the process of YTH ministry is to take God out of the process of YTH ministry and it becomes simply a natural organization or club or group. But the church and its ministries is not only natural, it is supernatural and exists within God.

So, to understand theology is where we start. Theology is simply the study of God.

Looking at the clearest definition is best seen in the following reference. The Strong's Concordance cites the term this way; *theos*: God, original word: θεός, οῦ, ὁ. Part of speech: Noun, feminine; Noun, masculine. Phonetic spelling: (theh'-os). The Strong's reference number is 2316 *(theós)* of unknown origin – properly, God, the Creator and owner of all things (Jn 1:3; Gen 1 - 3). Long before the New Testament was written, 2316 *(theós)* referred to the supreme being who owns and sustains all things. (2)

The other part of this word is *ology:* a word-forming element indicating a branch of knowledge. Originally used c 1800 in nonce formations or the study of something. When placed at the end of a word it denotes the study of that word or concept.

Psalm 78

One of the foundational texts in the scriptures on YTH ministry is found in Psalm 78.

I like to call Psalm 78 the generation's chapter. The word generations is specifically mentioned at least four times and alluded to another six or seven times in the chapter. It is the handoff from one generation to the next. It is sustainability. It is about the importance of the message of God for all time and reviews Israel's history detailing some very important messages. You'll recognize the language when you read it at the end of the book. Some of the language is iconic to scripture.

At the end of this book I have placed a simple commentary on Psalms 78. I've taken the chapter and broken it down into sections and given my slightly educated theological commentary for each section. But here, let me tell you why I have chosen Psalm 78 as a theological text for the support of YTH ministry.

This chapter is a review of Israel's history under David. As you know, most of the Psalms were written by David himself. This Psalm was written by Asaph, one of David's scribes, as he chronicles David's leadership over Israel. The entire chapter is a review of David's influence and growth as a young leader early in his Kingship and through to his impact in his latter years. It really is quite remarkable to hear the iconic phrases Asaph uses to review David's life.

There are two narratives in Psalm 78.

The first narrative Asaph speaks of in Psalm 78 is the message itself.

I want the message of God to be central in my personal life and in my public life. I want people to look at me and see the narrative of God by the way I live. I want them to see truth, grace, and love in all that I think, say, and do. Because the message is what I am passing on to the next generation. The message is the narrative and the theology of God

I want my students to see me walk up in front of them carrying a Bible rather than me alluding to it on the screen. I want my students to hear me quote the word in my message. Look at all the different ways Asaph defined the word of God and the message. We cannot lose the message. The message is the strength of the church. As a YTH pastor we must be constantly thinking of the message. If we are spending more time thinking about culture, coffee shops, and clothes we have lost the message.

> *The message is supernatural. Over the years, I have found the world is familiar with the supernatural, but, the church is foreign to it. Almost like we apologize for the supernatural. I have recently counted all of the movies and television shows playing in America based on the supernatural. There are no less than 19 that allude to the supernatural in their title. If you include the content of the movie or show the number swells to over 33 that are running right now.*

This is a significant trait of this generational set. Why is this so important?

Asaph defined the message by using words like *sayings of old*, *commandments*, *law*, *statutes*, *covenant*, and *testimonies*. This message is not only about words though. This message is about works. Another set of words he uses is *works*, *praises*, *wonders*, and *signs*. It is not just about *principle* it is about *power*. Our message is both word and works. We must not only speak the word of God to this generation, but, we must show the power of God's word to this generation. I believe young people need to see a demonstration of God in their generation.

Good theology is as much a *demonstration* of God as it is a *definition* of God.

The Millennial and the Gen Z set are totally into the supernatural. While the world is *familiar* with the supernatural the church is *foreign* to the supernatural. It really is simple. The supernatural is the act of God in human kind from Genesis to our time. I want my students to see the acts of God and not just hear about the past. This is where Psalm 78 and the generational traits of the Millennial and Gen Z become tandem are almost like the theology of the message of Psalm 78 is the place we should build our theology of YTH ministry.

> *Theology really is easy. If you've ever wondered what to preach on in YTH ministry this would be it. The acts and works of God! If all we did was spend an entire quarterly series bragging on God and His works and His word it would mesmerize a generation. They would be so attracted to His nature and character if we could define him to them.*

The second narrative Asaph speaks of in Psalm 78 is the sustainability of the message.

What is very clear in Psalm 78 is that there are several levels of people who must lead the responsibility of theological sustainability – that the message of God is dependent upon one generation sharing the narrative of God to the next generation.

A thorough read of this chapter finds the responsibility of theological sustainability falls to grandfathers and grandmothers, fathers and mothers, spiritual leaders, and an older generation of siblings telling of the ways of God to the next generation. Asaph was saying theology must begin in the home. Suffice it to say, the family cannot place the responsibility of theology solely on the church. The family must see itself at the center of biblical training. That makes one of the key roles of the YTH leader to help parents with the spiritual formation of their children.

> *When you look at the breakdown of the family you then begin to realize why only 4% of Gen Z has a biblical worldview. We can scream at the church all we want for its lack of theology, but, there is just no way teens are going to develop a biblical worldview when they haven't been told of one growing up in their home.*

The principles of one generation become the practices of the next.

So, if one generation loses its biblical principles, where will the next generation get theirs? Aside from the responsibility of the home in YTH theology in Psalm 78, Asaph's message on sustainability extends to the role of spiritual leaders – including YTH ministry leaders – defining God to this generation. Church leadership is part of the forefathers and the spiritual leaders Asaph talks about who prepare a generation.

In that light, I want to ask you a few simple questions concerning our spiritual heritage we are leaving to this generation:

1. What is your personal discipline as it comes to reading the word of God?
2. What is your personal discipline as it relates to studying the word of God?
3. Have you seen a new characteristic or trait of God in your personal spiritual life? Or have you continued to use the same language in defining God?
4. Do our students sense in us a love for the Word?
5. Are miracles, signs, and wonders happening in the YTH ministry?
6. Are my messages and series built around a cultural theme or a biblical theme?
7. When I counsel or give advice to students do I consult with the word of God?
8. Are my students a part of the 33% of teenagers in the church who can only name half of the 10 Commandments?

These are not easy questions.

But they demonstrate the importance of theology as a critical sustainability strategy for the church – beginning in the life of the family members at home, extended family members, spiritual leaders, and YTH leaders. Sustainability is the central and primary responsibility of the home. But it is clear every generation has a responsibility also. Psalm 78 is a very clear description of the activity of God in history. I do not want to be a YTH leader who leaves out the activity of God in 21st-century YTH ministry.

Let me give you a second text for a theology of YTH ministry and why we do what we do.

Matthew 18

These are Jesus' famous words about NextGen ministry.

Can you see the setting? Jesus is with the disciples teaching after His transfiguration. While He is teaching on the death and the resurrection and on paying taxes, one of the disciples asked Jesus, "Who then is the greatest in the kingdom of heaven?" A pretty random question in this moment. But look at what is going on in this moment and take yourself back to this scene.

There must've been some children playing nearby. Because the narrative takes a turn.

As Jesus is talking to the disciples, one of the children's frisbees was thrown up next to the disciples and they were distracted. Maybe the children were making too much noise and the disciples were hushing the children so they could hear what Jesus was saying. So Jesus answers their question about who is the greatest in the kingdom of heaven – *by calling a child over to his side.* No he did not ask Peter or John to come forward. He asked a middle school or elementary aged child to help Him answer their question. Now He has their attention.

> *Did you catch that thought!? Jesus defines the kingdom of God by bringing over a sixth grader. Ha ha. Now that is a theology of YTH ministry. You might be thinking I'm taking a stretch at this hermeneutic and commentary. Maybe a little. A little. Because this is a key word in the text.*

The Little One's

As we read this text further, Jesus answers them by saying, "I say to you, unless you are converted and become as a *little* child you cannot enter the kingdom of heaven." And Jesus isn't finished. He tells the disciples, who are young people themselves, that whoever hangs out with these *little* children is a friend of His. But wait, there's more. Jesus then warns them if they were to cause a *little* one to sin it would be better for him to be drowned in the depths of the sea. Finally, one more time, Jesus looks into their disdain and anger toward these *little* children being around and tells them, "Take heed that you do not despise one of these *little* ones."

This is not the only time Jesus dealt with this.

Remember, Jesus modeled this as a middle school aged adolescent when He stayed home from vacation and taught YTH group – or more accurately filled in for the Lead Pastor. The only teenage recording we have of Jesus in the Bible is Jesus as a student leader in church teaching the deacons and elders! Do you see? It's true. Not a stretch at all. Jesus spoke many times about the simplicity of the kingdom of God and children. We cannot define the kingdom of God without childlikeness.

We do not have the time to detail all of the young biblical leaders, but, the scriptures support a theology of the importance of YTH ministry throughout the Old Testament and the New Testament.

- Moses as a young deliverer and orphan boy who rose above Pharaoh
- Joshua serving under Moses as a teenager and learning how to become a great leader in his own right
- Joseph rising through all odds and finding favor with God and becoming the Prince of Egypt
- Esther and her girlfriends rescuing a generation of Jews
- Samuel as a young student in the Temple becomes a central prophet to King Saul and King David
- The succession model of kings and priests trusted the progeny of many kings and priests to turn the kingdom over to young leaders
- David rising above all others as the teenage king of Israel and lineage of the Messiah
- Josiah serving as king of Israel as a child and teen
- Daniel and his three friends being chosen above all the young men in the province
- Jeremiah the teenage prophet and his rise to influence with Josiah the King – what a tandem that was in history
- The New Testament priority of the rabbinical model of adolescent instruction
- Mary being chosen as a teenage virgin to birth the messiah
- Paul and his theology of mentoring and parenting YTH such as Timothy
- And of course Jesus defining the Kingdom with children as the example, and, choosing several teenagers as His disciples

Programming and Presence

I believe the central task of a YTH leader is not to merely build a *program* or culture but to strategically build a *presence* in scripture.

The primary task of a YTH leader is discipleship – that is, to preach *and* teach. There is no greater responsibility we have than this because the present condition we find ourselves in concerning YTH ministry is proof that preaching and teaching has taken a back seat in YTH ministry for too long. I am not saying organization and programming are not important. Hear me clearly. Organization and programming are important – but they are not primary. They are secondary. Preaching and teaching theology to the children is the primary task of the YTH leader.

In a recent commentary, R. Albert Mohler, the president of the Southern Baptist Theological Seminary in Louisville, KY, talks about the vital theological task performed by the pastor within the local Church:

"The pastoral calling is inherently theological. Given the fact the pastor is to be the teacher of the Word of God and the teacher of the Gospel, it cannot be otherwise. That teaching is done on both the congregational setting and a personal one as the body watches the pastor and his (or her) faith in action. The idea of the pastorate as a non-theological office is inconceivable in light of the New Testament." (3)

Pastor here is not dependent upon credentials or title or pay. This is calling. And every YTH leader has this responsibility at the center of their work. Mohler stresses the pastor's stewardship of the theological task requires a clear sense of pastoral priority. This must be foundational to the pastoral ministry of the local Church, and our ministry must emerge from a fundamentally theological foundation. Whether we as pastors and leaders are preaching, teaching, leading, planning, or counseling, our theology will guide our methodology.

One of my favorite descriptions of Pastoral Ministry is from Francis Chan, a contemporary author and Church planter in San Francisco. Chan has had a great impact on a new ecclesiology of Christianity over the past 5 years as he has been teaching and modeling a 1st century biblical and pastoral theology to the 21st century.

Chan's influence is noteworthy in this discussion because he recently stepped down as lead pastor of a mega-church in California to devote his life and ministry to helping the church value the process of discipleship at the local church level. A difficult task in this era of self-help religion and microwave Christianity. In the same article Chan goes on to say:

> *"...ministry looks like Acts 2 practices such as extended prayer, radical love and service, and intimate fellowship within the home. But technology is really about speed: doing everything faster and with less effort. We're tempted to want the*

> Church to be the same way—let me accomplish what I want in as little time as possible. But the blessing is going to come from the work itself, from the hard work you do to love and serve one another."

Look at the many definitions for Pastoral Theology:

Merriam-Webster completes their understanding of Pastoral theology as *"The study of the theological bases, as well as, the practical implications of the professional activities of religious workers."* (4)

Oxford Living Dictionary defines it as *"Christian theology that considers religious truth in relation to spiritual needs."* (5)

The Catholic Encyclopedia says Pastoral Theology is *"... the science of the care of* souls." (6)

Bible Study Tools differentiates Biblical theology from Pastoral theology as *"Practical or Pastoral theology focuses on Pastoral practices of Biblical truths in modern life."* (7)

The Gospel Coalition and Dave McDonald define Pastoral Theology as *"...Biblical gospel-shaped teaching and modeling the practices of God's word in people's lives, to lead God's people by the word of God's grace into eternity with God."* (8)

Developing a philosophy of ministry is critical to every young spiritual leader. Whether volunteer or paid YTH leader, every young leader must define for themselves how they are going to do the work of pastoring this generation. Philosophy and methodology will guide your YTH ministry on the daily journey of building a culture. Therefore, beginning with the definitions is an important first step in the process of defining your personal ministry philosophy.

A 4% Biblical Worldview

According to Barna in the Impact 360 Study from February 2018, only 4% of Gen Z has a biblical worldview. (9)

Wow. Just think about this. I didn't believe it when I heard it. This means 4% of teens in America think Christian. With Christian doctrine in mind and as a lens by which they see everything else in life. In a very real sense, it is when Christians live out their most fundamental beliefs in everyday life. This is what we would call a biblical worldview. How the Bible affects the way we think and everything we do.

Can you see how important the theology of YTH ministry is now? What have we done – or not done – to take our young people to these lowly depths of theological formation? I think this very well proves the essential task of the YTH pastor is to teach the students and to assist them to think theologically, in order to demonstrate discernment and authentic discipleship in their daily lives.

> *The YTH pastor must give attention, study, and time to the theological dimensions of ministry. A ministry that is deeply rooted in the truths of God's Word will be one of great success. A ministry that is deeply rooted in the ideology of God's World will be one of great failure. We must place scripture above culture.*

The YTH pastor's concentrated attention to the biblical and theological task is necessary for the establishment of his or her personal life. But also to the life of the YTH group. So not only the pastor, but also, the people, can learn to live out their most effective and authentic faith in culture with the most impact. This deposit of the biblical worldview will be done through the YTH pastor's faithful preaching, worship, discipleship, evangelism, and relationships in the Church and the local community.

Let's take a look at theology and YTH ministry in a different light.

Developing a Theology *in* YTH ministry

As a YTH leader and part of the pastoral leadership of the Church, whether full-time or volunteer, we must have the same commitment to theology lead pastor's must have. Dare I say we must have more of an emphasis?

With the brokenness of the family and the lack of spirituality in the family in America, we are graduating our young people into adulthood empty of theology. Theology is the first responsibility of parents and guardians. But let's face it, we have a lot of work to do to make that happen. So maybe starting with a new set of parents – our teenagers – is the quickest way to get there.

Because of our responsibility of raising the Next Gen in the church, we have a great role in shaping the biblical worldview of our students. This role will be successful if we can define our philosophy and culture of ministry – a philosophy of theology and a culture of love. What I mean by this is that our YTH culture should not be a cool vibe, slick marketing, current trends, and solid worship teams. Our YTH ministry culture should scream theology!

Maybe the reason the biblical theology statistics among Gen Z are so low is because we have for the most part left the Bible and theology out of YTH ministry the last 20 years. Wherever this is happening, and if this is happening, that is a critical mistake. To think the church would lessen the study of God in YTH ministry is a growing reality as leaders minor on theology and major on *meology*.

Could it be the reason students are not serving God is because students do not know God? And the reason they do not know God is because they are not being taught theology at the YTH ministry level. If there is no theological culture in YTH ministry then we are graduating students who have a 4% biblical worldview.

Pamela Erwin, in her book "A Critical Approach to Youth Culture", speaking of Karl Barth's cultural theology views, gives four criteria for evaluating culture in YTH ministry:

1. Have our works led to student's freedom or to their greater bondage?
2. Have our works uplifted students a little or thrust them deeper into the mire?
3. Have our works united students or divided them from the whole church?
4. Have our works built up or thrown down, gathered or scattered, quickened or slain?
    (10)

I would add three more criteria for evaluating theology in YTH culture to this list by Erwin:

5. Have our works increased the knowledge of biblical content in our students?
6. Have our works practically taught and caused our students to share their faith?
7. Have our works brought transformation in the lives of our students?

This is an interesting look at how theology is built, and, how to measure theology in the YTH setting. Every YTH leader should look at these questions and measure our culture of theology in the YTH group.

Here are 5 practical ways to place theological strength at the center of the YTH leader:

1. Personally dedicate at least 20 hours weekly to the spiritual disciplines.

Included in this commitment would be sitting under the preaching and teaching of the Word, watching videos or listening to podcasts, reading the Bible, fasting, prayer, and your personal study time. Each of these can give you a biblical education.

This is one practice of mine that has driven my children's ministry, my YTH ministry, the years I spent as an evangelist, our church planting years, my teaching ministry at the university level, and now my writing. If you do not schedule significant time in the Word of God and the spiritual disciplines, the ideology of the culture will shape your ministry. That is a dangerous place to be.

I have a set time of spiritual discipline. I don't add it when I'm free. For me, it is the same time every evening. Every morning. And nothing gets in the way of it.

2. Annually attend a conference on ministry.

Some of the greatest moments in my 35 years of ministry have been at these conferences. District events, YTH Conferences, Billy Graham Evangelistic Conference, National Youth Workers Conference, Society for Pentecostal Studies meetings, Ministerial retreats, and even a scholarly reading online class. Learning from other people who have made theology their life's pursuit is a quick education for you.

In the conference setting learning from theology or field professionals can remove the lid and the fences from your personal life that exist because of our created patterns of rote learning from the same source.

76

Barna Research posted in their Impact 360 study of 2018 that only 29% of pastors attend a conference on ministry annually. I stress to YTH leaders that one conference a year will keep them from getting behind in their theology and help them keep current in field. One of the great moments in my early years of YTH ministry happened in a conference setting and is still impacting my ministry today – and it took place more than 30 years ago.

3. Personally build relationships with a YTH pastor or leader outside of your theological bend.

A monthly mentoring meeting will yield great results from one great mind to another. Another opportunity similar to this would be to involve yourself in the area ministerial association. You will experience great conversation from all kinds of theological world views around breakfast or lunch. One of the great benefits you get from ecumenical relationships is an understanding of other's theology and how that might be shaping students under their ministry.

I have learned new language meeting with a Catholic YTH leader, understood the rich tradition of a Methodist YTH leader, and had powerful conversations with my Baptist YTH leader friends about salvation in preaching.

4. Try an online or local university course in theology.

It is inexpensive and educational to take a New Testament or Old Testament course or even an Eschatology course to keep us fresh. Maybe your church will even pay for it.

Theology and life really are symbiotic. The marriage of biblical matters and everyday life for teens is crucial to the building of the kingdom of God. Without accurate and practical biblical teaching, YTH ministry will be under-developed and ineffective against the rise of post-modern thought that exists in the public schools. Sound practical principles can protect your pursuit of biblical authority as a YTH pastor.

Take your study and theology seriously and you will see supernatural spiritual formation and depth in your personal life, and, in the students of your YTH ministry. Trust me, this spiritual discipline to take an online course will challenge your marriage and family as well..

5. Make sure your messaging and series are based in the Bible.

We cannot simply base our preaching and teaching in cultural happenings or current affairs. That is a changing milieu. There must be a balance between *'the newspaper and the Bible'* in preaching and teaching – and preferably leaning toward the Bible!

A very practical way to do this would be to make sure your title images or series promo has a text on it. You could also accomplish this by having your first words as you are beginning your message to students be a reference to the text. Something like "go to the book of John as we begin this message".

> *Maybe the reason why only 33% of teenagers in the church can name only half of the Ten Commandments is because YTH ministry has done a poor job of theology. Maybe the reason why only 14% of people in America read the Bible daily is because the Church has done a poor job of raising its children around the excitement of a systematic theology of God.*
>
> *Maybe the reason why teenagers today do not list spiritual leaders or pastors within the top 10 of 'guides on moral issues' is because as YTH leaders we have lost our theological authority in this culture and replaced it with meology.*

After all, the only people who do not serve God are people who do not know God.

As we said at the beginning of this chapter, students have been under-challenged by YTH ministry in America. We must make it a priority to introduce God to teenagers again. This is best done through theology. It is our simple responsibility to define God to a generation and watch them chase after Him.

Students are much more able to handle knowledge than we think. We need to capitalize on the educational achievement and competitiveness of the Millennial and Gen Z set. Because students are focused upon scholarship amidst the high cost of education, this proves to us how able students are too receive instruction and knowledge.

It is the responsibility of YTH leadership to raise a generation of young people who are literate in biblical theology. So what does that look like? What are the universal things we should want every teen to understand?

The Theological Non-negotiables for Teens

As YTH leaders we must be Christian and not merely American in our theology. The Bible is our constitutional source for values and ethics and not the U.S. Constitution.

The Lord's Prayer begins with "Our father which art in heaven" - not "Our father which art in Washington, or in New York, or in LA". To understand God solely through culture is dangerous because culture is shifting and temporary. It will define God within a humanistic framework. God is best understood through scripture because scripture is not shifting, it is eternal. Let me explain the theological solution for YTH today through the Christian worldview.

Teenagers are void of theology in the 21st century.

According to Barna in the Impact 360 Study from February 2018 that we introduced earlier in this chapter, only 4% of Gen Z has a biblical worldview. That number has dropped significantly in each of the last three generational sets. So, it is imperative we re-introduce God to this generation. For a decade now we have seen the rise of the 'none's' (those with no faith) and the 'SBNR' (Spiritual But Not Religious) groups who have no Christian theological framework. And the only way to stop this slide is theology training of a generation in YTH ministry.

> *It shouldn't concern you whether you have the best ga-ga ball pit or 9-square cage in your area. Our greatest concern is not the newest foam machine game or the hottest new carnival YTH event. If you are able to do all of this and theology, great! But, what should concern you most is how many of my students understand who God is. How many of my students are learning principles in the Bible. How comfortable my students are with prayer, worship, studying God's word, and apologetics or sharing their faith.*

We must have non-negotiable theological specifics because the Millennial and Gen Z set have no framework for theology because it wasn't passed down to them. They may be the truly 'post-Christian' generation in America we have talked about for years. An accurate theology of God and man is critical for teenagers – that begins with an accurate interpretation and understanding of the Bible in the YTH ministry setting.

So what does that look like? How do we evaluate whether we have adequate theology in YTH ministry?

I think these are an easy set of questions to answer. You may have your own important things and elementary content you feel is essential for teenagers to learn in your setting. That's good. Make a list and have a strategy each year with themes that will address this content with regular quarterly assessment.

I am asked this question about theological topics and content often. So here is my non-negotiable list of the things every teenager should learn once they have left our YTH ministry:

Biblical Content

The Ten Commandments, The Sermon on the Mount material (what I like to call the New Testament Commandments), Key Bible Stories throughout the Old and New Testaments, The Gospels, Paul & basic theology of grace and truth from the Epistles, The Fruit of the Spirit, The Gifts of the Spirit, End-Times Eschatology and Apocalyptic theology, and basic Apologetics - How to share their faith.

What does that look like specifically? Here is a way to break down the content specifically:

The Ten Commandments – As the universal basis for all human life and contact, the Ten Commandments must be the critical elementary and foundational emphases in YTH ministry. These change everything.

Key Bible Stories – Our students need general Biblical knowledge. Such as the stories from the Old and New Testament. This would include the Creation Account, the life of Joseph, Jonah, Joshua, Job, David, Elijah and Elisha, the story of Daniel, the Gospel miracles and parables, the life of Paul, the Book of Acts and the beginnings of the Church, and The Revelation.

Sermon on the Mount – As important as the Ten Commandments of the Old Testament and the Law is to us, the Sermon on the Mount is also a critical part of our spirituality. Things like going one mile instead of two, giving our shirt and our coat, and turning the opposite cheek to someone who has hurt us. Just as the Ten Commandments are a way of life and practice for us, so also is the Sermon on the Mount. I call them the New Testament Commandments. They are practical teachings of Christ for life and practice today.

The Fruit and Gifts of the Spirit – I want my students to know what Jesus and Paul taught about the Holy Spirit and His impact upon my life. Our students know God the Father and God the Son. But who is the Holy Spirit? We must help them to become more familiar with His work in our lives. This includes walking in the Spirit and the development of the fruit in our lives. It also helps to know the power that comes from the gifts of the Spirit to empower us for works of service.

End-times and Apocalyptic Events – Having a grasp of the final days and the future of mankind and the world is very hopeful. We must make The Revelation become more than a symbolic book of the bible. The incredible picture of heaven and the scenes of our future and blessed hope is powerful. There aren't a lot of things more important to teenagers than hope today. When you talk to teenagers, the future is powerful. Helping them to see their future will be very influential to their spiritual lives and ultimately their spiritual formation.

Simplistic isn't it? Yet we need some kind of measurement.

These basic biblical content of Christianity will help us define God to a generation that does not know Him. Actually, theology really is simple. I believe theology is the missing key in YTH ministry. As YTH leaders, if we can introduce our students to God, I have no question they will serve Him. Because the only people who do not *serve* God are people who do not *see* God. Accurate theology is where *The Next (Third) Great Awakening* begins. To see the Millennial and Gen Z set awakened to who God actually is.

In addition to the biblical content, here are a few spiritual disciplines every student must be taught before they leave our YTH ministry:

Spiritual Disciplines

Prayer – Our students know they should pray. But, if our students are not taught how to pray we have failed them. Teach them daily themes, weekly prayer time, monthly topics, an annual retreat, and a lifetime of commitment to praying at any time.

Scripture – Regular biblical reading and study. We have established in this book the vital role of theology in YTH ministry. But here is a little more practical help on this - Reading partners, YouVersion App, encouraging teens to set alarms and notifications on their phones, scripture memorization, and reading out-loud.

Fasting – To a generation that is selfish this is a powerful principal that will take their spiritual lives to the next level. Choose one meal a week and one day a month. Create a fasting time for the whole YTH group. We have over a thousand teenagers fasting and praying on Fridays at lunch!

Worship – We don't have to teach this generation to worship. We need to teach this generation how to worship God. This can be done through a series, nights of worship, and giving worship a priority in the YTH service on a regular basis.

Giving – God set the highest example and gave his only Son. His servants should do the same. What can our students give to? They can give time, talent, and money to local causes, global causes, home/foreign missions, peer's needs, or humanitarian campaigns.

Apologetics – How can someone believe unless they hear? Our students need to know not only what they believe but they need to know how to share it. Can the news be that *Good* if it's not heard? It is not enough to tell our students they have to share their faith. We must teach them how to share their faith and reach their friends. That may look like how to have transitional statements with their friends that lead to faith conversations, knowing their personal story in 1 minute, or having a basic understanding of apologetics.

Justice – A desire for biblical and social justice is one of the most important needs in the world today. We need to teach our students they can make a difference in race relations and social justice. Teach them the language of reparation and healing: intersectionality (we cannot interact in isolation of each other), identity development (holistic teaching of self-worth), reparations (complete personal and public compensation for harm), privilege (unearned advantage), forgiveness, prejudice (negative unsupported attitudes), reconciliation (restorative attitude and behavior), movement building (the effort of social change agents to engage power holders and the broader society in addressing a systemic problem or injustice while promoting an alternative vision or solution.

Action Steps

Try these practical ways to increase theology in YTH ministry:

- *We must use the Bible as YTH Leaders as the base of our preaching and teaching and the content of planned small group ministry*
- *Every YTH leader should use a physical copy of the Bible in YTH settings when they are teaching or preaching*
- *Ask students to bring their bibles to YTH and asking them to use their bibles during messaging. The YouVersion Bible App should be secondary to students bringing a bible.*
- *Training students to study the bible on their own – creating a setting and a time and place to read and pray, starting with proverbs daily, reading through the gospels for general information and important words of Jesus, and encouraging students to attend a bible study at their school*
- *What is co-dependency in our students? How do our students demonstrate this? Talk through the ways to breaking co-dependency of the YTH Ministry and the student by teaching students to serve God in their context and not just at church.*
- *How can we help students become dependent upon God and not YTH ministry?*
- *Make sure that our small group settings are charged with biblical content, strong leadership, worship response, and not just simply random discussion groups*
- *Providing theological content for students to use on Social Media to promote the current YTH group series. Using sermon notes apps, graphics, memes, and posts of scriptural content that helps students redeem their Social platforms and promote the YTH ministry.*
- *Encouraging students to turn their bedrooms into prayer rooms with worship playlists, reading plans, letting their family know when they are doing their spiritual disciplines, and listening to a podcast weekly*

"Fads swept the YTH of the sprawl at the speed of light;
entire subcultures could rise overnight,
thrive for a dozen weeks,
and then vanish utterly."
— William Gibson, Neuromancer

Chapter 4

Trends in YTH Ministry

The problem we face today is that the church has come late to the party called Millennials – and now the church is in danger of completely missing the party called Gen Z.

I have the advantage of seeing YTH Ministry in a variety of settings across our nation. It is an honor to sit with leaders and students across our nation in the church, para-church, school, and organizational settings. To be honest, sitting with YTH leaders across our nation is one of the reasons I cannot stop doing this! It is an education in itself.

How is that?

YTH Ministry comes in different shapes, sizes, colors, personalities, attitudes, backgrounds, and even faiths. Every setting, whether urban or suburban or rural, or, whether in the small or medium or large church. Even the para-church context. Every setting is unique because every leader has ways or philosophies or a model on how to do ministry depending on the setting and the culture they are in, or, depending on their personal framework and experience from their own YTH ministry days as a teenager.

It can be easy for a YTH leader to assume all of YTH ministry is exactly like the setting they are in. When in actuality, YTH ministry is localized and distinct. However, the one constant is the generation we are trying to reach and they should be at the heart of our theological and cultural framework.

They call them Gen Z. Here's a description from Barna and the Impact 360 Study from 2018:

> *"We've been talking for years about Millennials. But now a new generation is becoming a cultural force in their own right—and it's time to pay attention. Born between 1999-2015 (Ages 2-18) Gen Z has a population size of 69-70 million and is just now beginning to enter college. The major lifetime events for the Gen Z include the invention of Facebook (2004), the Apple debut of the iPhone (2007), the election of Barack Obama (2008), a huge financial crisis (2008), the legalization of gay marriage (2015), and the election of Donald Trump (2016)."* (1)

I would add the rise in school shootings and the dissension in government to this influential list of formative life moments in a teenager's life. Both of these have shaped their world in significant ways over the past 2-3 years.

The Greatest Sociologists

No matter our philosophy of YTH ministry we must become the greatest sociologists on the planet or we will be in danger of losing the platform we need to introduce this new generation to God and the church. It is going to take an informed effort to bridge the gap between this present generation, their world, God, and the church. Because of the chasm fixed between these, it will take an effort of intention and strategy on our part, and, a heavenly surprise visitation on God's part.

What is undeniable are the things I see first-hand across America as broad-based characteristic traits of the YTH culture. Here are 7 trends I see impacting how we do YTH ministry to the Millennial and the Gen Z set in America.

I understand I have a lens I view everything from. It is my worldview or framework of YTH ministry and how I got here through my background and upbringing. I understand this book is charged with my ways or leans gathered over the years. Use these observations to help you as a leader to define your own philosophy or model or way of doing YTH ministry.

Especially with the following current trends in mind.

The Disintegration of the Family

One of the glaring negative trends in our society right now is the disintegration of the family. This is no secret. We have lost the family structure in America and much of what we are dealing with in the wake of this is not good. We need YTH leaders to step up and fix this by playing our part in raising the next great father's and mother's and sister's and brother's.

If we don't stop this negative trend, it will only get worse. Capitalize on this moment and seize the day. When things are worse, that is when a culture producer steps up! Just like David, Esther, Daniel, Mary, Jesus, and Paul, each of us as YTH leaders must position ourselves so the Spirit will come upon us and we can impact our generation. We have to do the same things today to shape our culture that great men and women have done through the ages to shape their culture.

For YTH leaders in the 21st century, if we are going to shape our culture it will begin with the family.

Here's our current issue: We are not just raising a fatherless generation anymore. We are raising a motherless and a siblingless generation. Students do not know their family system.

This is not to say every classic or traditional family with biological parents in the home is perfect, or, that every blended or mixed family with non-biological parents in the home is broke. But what we need is healthy homes in every family structure whether classic or blended. The reason for this is because the condition of our society has mirrored the condition of the family.

> *Something I've learned over the years is that the best kids do not always come from the best homes. And the worst kids do not always come from the worst homes. In fact, the opposite has been true also. I have seen the best kids come from the worst homes and the worst kids come from the best homes!*

There are many reasons for this. Every parent is different, every child is different, every experience in the home is different, and every community around the family is different. Some teens are more resilient than others. One more thing I've learned is that family is not an equation. Raising a healthy home is not math. It is art!

The traditional family is no longer the norm. We used to live in families where biological parents and children were customary, where siblings took care of and corrected themselves, and the grandparents were an extra set of eyes around the house! I can remember my older sister looking out for me, and, in turn, me looking out for my younger brothers. Maybe it was not always in their best interest but it certainly was in mine! I mean, I could beat them up and pound on them, but I would not let anyone else do that.

I have watched the outcomes from broken homes cripple teens. It may be the number 1 problem in their world. We will talk about the sexual revolution, the social media phenomenon, and the loss of a biblical worldview. But it is unquestionably the family that is the thermostat of society and every culture.

The reason I say this is because if the family is healthy then we are raising teenagers who can deal with any of the other problems and issues in society we could talk about. So let me encourage you with some practical ways to improve the ministry marriage and ultimately the home our children will grow up in.

Before my wife passed away in 2015, Jane and I put together our *Top Ten Ways to Improve Our Marriage and Home*. Nobody has a perfect marriage. But here's our attempt to create better ministry marriages and homes and to stop this disastrous trend. I've included 5 for this chapter.

1. Listen

It sounds so simple, but it is true. How do you feel when you know you are really being listened to? How do you feel when you know you are not being listened to? See the difference? Trying to listen to someone while you are on social media or while you watch the TV is not listening. I know our children want to have family dinner and devotions at the table. They may say the opposite, but, deep down inside, they would love it! Because they would be heard.

Our students are watching our marriages and families. They are watching how we relate to each other as a couple. They will notice when we look them in the eye and let them talk. Modeling listening places value on someone else's life. It will create a family atmosphere and environment in the YTH ministry when a YTH leader shows up and is interested in a teenagers life by simply listening to them.

I do not remember where I found this statistic, and I have been asked several times the last few years. But I ran across a stat stating U.S. fathers spend only 18 minutes weekly speaking face to face with their child. If this is true, it sheds alarming light on the condition of our society.

2. Apologize

I heard of the husband who would apologize to his wife at the beginning of the week – for all of the stupid things he would do in the coming days that week. It was a humorous thing but it broke the ice I'm sure. Apologize every evening when you go to bed. In any relationship, you will have something for which to apologize. A genuine apology communicates that you care enough about the other person to admit when you are wrong and try not to do it again.

Our teenagers are living in a world buried under guilt and condemnation. That guilt and condemnation can be broken by leaders who model apologetic living in front of them. How many times have you said the words, "I'm sorry"? People need to hear us say this. Apologetic living sets an atmosphere of forgiveness and levity for everyone to sense.

3. Compliment

This cannot be overstated. Appreciation goes a long way to setting a healthy secure environment. The family should be the most secure place on earth where everyone can be themselves and ask questions and feel no judgment. Encouragement and appreciation can also help bring identity in the home. When a parent speaks over a child and affirms or labels a child with prophetic identity, it can be one of the most defining conversations in a child's life. I always spoke over my kids that they were loved, they couldn't do anything to change that, and that they were going to change the world.

Our students are run on the fuel of exhortation.

Think about the YTH ministry setting and this idea of complimenting. If a student comes to YTH time and again and are told they are loved and nothing can change that, they will be back. Why? Because this is not how the world treats people. The world teenagers are growing up in is conditional. The church should be unconditional.

I truly believe if we speak prophetically into a teenager's life it will counter the negative words spoken over them and they will be back again next week. A family environment that is complimenting and affirmative and encouraging is the perfect seedbed for adolescents to grow in.

Be specific. You can always compliment their physical appearance, their dress, or shirt, or haircut. But, you can go farther than the outward with the following: "*I really like the way you handled that situation", "You are such a good example to the other students", or, "You are going to do great things for God."* Take the time to speak identity over students and watch the increase in positivity and also in your attendance.

4. Tactile love

Touch, hold, caress - How well the family does this may be the most powerful affect upon the identity and the sexuality of our children.

I have had so many conversations with students who have broken relationships with their parents and many times the conversation led to a lack of affection in the home. Everyone needs to be touched. When I work with couples who are having problems, one of the very first things I suggest is to simply hold each other. When I have done this, it breaks the atmosphere in the room. Affection is a game-changer. That one small move contributes to a great deal of healing in a relationship and touch is a great way to build the entire family relationship.

Our students do not need YTH leaders to be their parent because they need healing of that relationship where it applies. But, with the disintegration of the family, if YTH leaders would model healthy homes in front of students then YTH ministry becomes much more effective.

Let me say we do not only need touch in the home, but, we need more of this in YTH ministry also. I know, I know. We live in a litigious society and we have to stick with the "side hug". I understand this. But, listen for a moment.

> *Many more leaders have left ministry because of a **lack** of affection and proper or principled love to their students than the leaders who have failed because of an **excess** of improper affection and lust.*

We must have practices that protect our principles. If we do not have best practices, our principles may not be very important to us. Please don't be afraid and don't be dissuaded to love people through gestures with pure motives such as handshakes, side hugs, or putting your hand on someone's arm. If your heart is right then your gesture will be also. I understand the risk here and we are living in a society that misreads everything, but, we cannot in reaction become sterile.

In our YTH ministry, we truly wanted to show teenagers they were going to be loved if they came to our YTH ministry. Over the years, I have had students tell me this kind of loving environment saved them from the negative attention from a lust-filled and power-seeking relationship of another peer or adult. All because our students knew they could get a godly hug and a "holy kiss" from a YTH pastor and leaders and peers who loved them with integrity if they came to our YTH ministry.

5. Family devotions

One of the most important things a ministry family can do at home is to center itself around the Bible, worship, and prayer. I did not want my kids to have two fathers – a father at church and another father at home. I wanted to be the same person when I was leading others as I was while I was leading my family.

This may seem like an unrealistic statement, but, the family that prays together stays together. Families in society are falling apart so it is imperative ministry families model a healthy home and thrive together. Especially for teenagers and young adults who are the offspring of unhealthy traditional or nontraditional families.

Modeling Practical Spiritual Discipline in the Home

In short, it begins with family devotion and faith that might look like seasonal family outreach such as food kitchens or service projects, weekly prayer at the family table, worship in the living room with a sweet playlist, reading and story time with the kids before bed, or even sitting together in church as a family. It is important to set early patterns of spiritual discipline in the home because it will become almost impossible to do that once the children become older.

There are a lot of ways ministry families can become great examples for a generation with such broken marriages and families. But elementary to this is theology in the home. I wanted my kids to learn theology in the home – that is why we taught them the Ten Commandments. That is why they had to sit through my preaching at dinner time. Or why they would sit through another video or book I would show them or read to them. I think at times my kids were completely bored.

Of course, we were creative, and there were many great moments, but, the family devotion dynamic takes work. My wife was very practical and added a lot of tactile lessons in our family devotion time. Whether it was dirt in the brownies, rotten apples in a lunch bag, broken lightbulbs, or some other object lesson Jane created, our family devotion time became a strength of our home.

> We cannot raise codependent children who merely serve God at church. Our devotions at home were regular and they were affective over the long-haul. Through the years, my kid's friends asked if they could come to our family devotions. Once they were in this atmosphere they were hooked. It became one of the ways our kids lived their faith outside of church.

Watching my kids learn to share or pray in family devotions was one of the reasons why I believe they have all chosen to be in ministry. Whatever reports they may have heard at the church, whatever things were said about mom and dad, and however our kids were treated by others, our kids new our home was the final word. My kids were getting a consistent message at home that could counter anything said outside of it.

When YTH leaders are modeling family devotion at home, students can sense the health. Especially if they do not come from a solid spiritual home. Because the majority of homes the teenagers are raised in are broken, a healthy YTH leader home becomes a huge asset in the YTH ministry.

With the growing disintegration of the family in our culture, we cannot allow YTH ministry to do the same. YTH ministry must model the priority of building a culture of family. That kind of culture in YTH ministry will be magnetic and bring about the healing needed in the Millennial and the Gen Z home today.

Here's another ascending trend in YTH ministry.

Emphasis on Theology

We have covered this topic in a previous chapter. But let me hit a few key points I see as a mounting trend in this generation. You may think I am talking about the loss of theology in YTH ministry. While that is definitely the case over the years, there is another mounting trend in this generation.

Theatre Versus Theology

It would be easy to state the negative here - that most YTH ministry is not valuing theology. As a matter fact, in too many settings, theater, and not theology, is the choice. But, I want to highlight the positive trend I see in many YTH ministries across the country. I see a rising emphasis of theology in YTH ministry today. The problem is it hasn't been there for too long, and, in too many settings, teenagers have been under-challenged spiritually by the church.

How long is it going to take to counter the 4% biblical worldview in our nation? Will the next generation increase their biblical worldview and grow to 10%? Or will it drop?

YTH ministry went through a season the last 15 years or so that became known more for theatre than for theology. It is hard to define but it is easy to see. The outcomes from YTH ministry the last 15-20 years have yielded very little disciple-making and it yielded far less young people being called into the office of ministry than the 20 years prior. If statistics like these are the outcomes from YTH ministry the last 20 years, we need some changes.

This trend can be seen in statistics like only one-third of Christian teenagers in America who can name half of the Ten Commandments, that Gen Z has the largest atheist adherents of all time, and, teenagers have ranked spiritual leaders outside of the top ten influential people in their lives.

Think about this! Only one-third of our students in the church can name 5 of the Ten Commandments. What has happened in our society where the most recent generation is the largest adherents to atheism? Maybe most compelling is that clergy have dropped out of the most influential people in a young person's life. Add to these disappointing trends the statistic shared throughout this book about Gen Z having a 4% biblical worldview and it becomes clear this data is simply outcomes of poor theology in YTH ministry and families the last two decades.

This lack of theology can also be seen in how the church treats its young people. In the public school system, there is a greater expectation, social relations, and an assumption for understanding depth of content toward teenagers than we have in the church. In too many settings, the church is treating young people 2-3 grades younger than they really are.

A Lack of Depth in YTH Preaching

YTH ministry has under-challenged teenagers.

Does the church realize how much adolescents are able to focus, get along with each other, and process information? I think we have underestimated young people. While the school system has increased expectations of teenagers, the church has lessened our expectations of teenagers.

With this approach it can be easy for YTH leaders to hesitate including the depth of theology in our messaging in the YTH service or discipleship programming while at the same time watering down our content. How many YTH ministries are stunting the spiritual growth of Junior High students by withholding from them a kind of "rights of passage" into the YTH ministry by delaying their spiritual formation because we think they are incapable of understanding theology?

Look at it like this.

- Teens in the public school are expected to be on time
- They are expected to turn in completed homework assignments done on their own
- Every day they must respect each other in class
- When a teacher or peer is talking they are challenged to listen in school
- School classes start on time
- Students are expected to have their textbooks with them

Compare these expectations to the ones we have for teenagers.

Do we start on time? Do we create messages and content they will take home? Is the YTH setting charged with honor and respect? Is our content challenging students to think about theology? Do we expect our students to come to YTH group with their bibles? Have you seen their homework?

I have a Master's Degree and do not understand material within a middle-schooler's concepts and glossary. We must set a more challenging environment in YTH ministry in the coming season. They can understand a lot more than we think. Looking at the biblical literacy in the Millennial and Gen Z sets, maybe the reason these statistics are so low is because we have left the bible and theology out of YTH ministry.

George Barna, in his 2005 study and book called *Revolution,* said that the needed transformation and awakening in society must start in the church. But the problem is, Barna wrote, *"...I was stunned and deeply disappointed at how relatively rare spiritual transformation instances were."* (2) What Barna was saying is that very little transformation is happening in the church. A lack of transformation in the church is a direct result of a lack of truth in the church.

It seems really simple to me actually. Theology is the study of God and if theology is missing in YTH ministry, then students are not serving God because students do not know God. Because as YTH leaders we have focused more upon meology than we have theology. From my travel and conversations, it is easy to see the validity of the data mined from research organizations like Barna, Pew, and others.

Where has this lack of theological depth come from? In my own estimation, I think the lack of theological depth in YTH ministry preaching has originated because of many things:

1. It all begins in the home – and our homes have lost the place of theology in raising our children
2. A previous generation of YTH leaders who built YTH ministry without the Bible at the center of it all
3. A previous generation of preachers who have devalued the Word of God and modeled to students poor homiletics and hermeneutics in their sermons
4. An over-emphasis upon programming and an under-emphasis upon presence in the YTH ministry and the church

5. The loss of theology in churches and YTH groups that may have missed out on discipling and developing students who were called to ministry - in the office setting of ministers and not just the field setting as Christians
6. An imbalance of deductive (direct preaching) and inductive (indirect preaching) approaches
7. Social Media, Tedtalks, podcasts, and the emergence of efficiency in communication has created "twitter speakers" or "one-liner" messages rather than a more expository message
8. An over-emphasis upon the presentation and style of the message or the messenger as the impetus for change and transformation
9. An under-emphasis upon the demonstration of the Spirit as the impetus for change and transformation
10. All of this resulting in an ideological meology or lack of personal spiritual discipline in shallow YTH leaders and preachers

One of the most obvious trends we see in preaching and teaching today is a lack of theology of the nature and character of God. We must be willing to speak more challenging content into the life of teenagers today. I truly believe the only teenager that does not *serve* God is the teenager who does not *know* God. Where there is a lack of teaching and preaching on the nature and character of God, there will be a lack of disciples in our YTH ministries.

> *Maybe the reason why only 14% of people in America read the bible daily is because the church has done a poor job of raising its children around the excitement of a systematic theology of God. Maybe the reason why 4% of Gen Z has a biblical worldview is because YTH ministry has failed for two decades to present a clear picture of God. Maybe the reason why only one-third of our students in the church can name only 5 of the Ten Commandments is because YTH ministry has failed the theology test.*

Theology is not an enemy of juvenialization. The next trend I see in American culture.

Juvenialization of YTH Ministry

In Peter Pan, the lost boys were separated from society because of their behavior. But the story is more than the symbolism of juvenile behavior and escapism. It really is more about parenting and valuing our children and the stage they are in as adolescents.

Juvenialization is the retaining by adults the traits from a previous generation or set. In its simplest definition some have called it childishness. But I want to use it a different way. I want to use it as childlikeness. Juvenialization does not have to be a sign of weakness in a generation. Is retaining traits from one set to another really a bad thing? I believe it depends upon the traits being retained. Maybe we should be concentrating on *childlike* traits of the younger generation. I'm not talking about retaining *childishness*. But, maybe at least promoting positive innocent childlike traits we see in our young people and teenagers.

We have seen that even Jesus defined the kingdom of God with children and He called the disciples to learn from the characteristic traits of the children playing around them. Theology is not an enemy of the adolescent. Every home could use a dose of juvenialization. It seems the older we get the more cynical we get. I don't believe theology is cynical. I think it is mystical and based upon the factual nature of God and childlike descriptions of God.

Some people have taken juvenialization to extremes and drawn unrealistic conclusions about young people and who they really are.

Merchants of Cool

This is a term for marketing and businesses who prey on the young. Our culture has this generation wrapped around its slick marketing ploy - that teenagers are simply quick twitch consumers and an easy target of materialistic companies. I know some of this might be true, but, it is only true in part. Young people are much deeper than "merchants of cool" think. The danger of juvenialization is thinking young people have been duped and led to the slaughter of culture wars. I believe their childlikeness is more mature than we think.

> *I think equally, culture has duped many adults, YTH leaders, and the church into thinking teenagers are whimsical and they cannot be taken serious. But this is simply not true. I cannot tell you how many times I have had students tell me they can handle truth, doctrine, and theology. And they want more!*

I will often pull students aside at a YTH setting and ask them if they understand me and my preaching or writing. In that moment I do not let them just nod their head. It is in these moments I hear students say to me they get it. I have at times even apologized for being too deep. Time and again, students have told me to bring it because they can handle it. More than not, I have had students telling me they want more depth in their YTH group!

Educational Aspirations and its Influence on Teenagers

This academic or competitive characteristic trait is actually a marker of this Millennial and Gen Z set and should challenge us as YTH leaders to give them more theology. We mentioned this earlier, but, because of the high cost of education and university, teens today are focused upon scholarship because they must be competitive and eligible to earn academic grants and funding to be able to afford school.

We need to capitalize on the educational achievement and competitiveness of the Millennial and Gen Z set by building our YTH ministries with a theological foundation founded upon scripture.

Do you see the fit?

This is a great reason why every YTH ministry should be emphasizing theology. Why every YTH leader should be challenging students with greater content. And why every YTH leader should be raising our expectations of teenagers and not lowering them! Remember the quote at the beginning of this chapter on trends. *"Fads swept the YTH of the sprawl at the speed of light; entire subcultures could rise overnight, thrive for a dozen weeks, and then vanish utterly."* Let the games vanish. But don't let theology vanish away.

As YTH leaders our challenge is that theology is not one of those fads or passing trends. But that theology doesn't, as William Gibson in Neuromancer states, "vanish utterly". We will discuss this further in the chapter on the future of YTH ministry.

The Identity Issue (Purpose and Purity/Sexuality)

Another trend in YTH ministry is the identity issue. We could define this trend in two streams.

First, as a *purpose* or destiny problem with teens and their relationship with the gospel. Second, we could define this as a *purity* or sexual revolution problem with teens and their relationship with gender.

I think they go together quite importantly. Both of these emphases have a lot to do with identity confusion. Confusion of our responsibility to the *gospel*, and, the confusion of our responsibility to our *gender*. Both of these issues are critical right now to teenagers. Maybe the question should be posed: What comes first? Spiritual identity or sexual identity?

Let's deal with a teenager's identity in Christ first. Because I believe this will shape a proper sexual identity.

The Spiritual Revolution (Purpose as Identity)

Think about it this way. When an adolescent finds their identity in Christ, they have everything they need to solve life's problems. When they are faced with the issues of life they are able to place them in the framework of who they are in Christ and not who they are in Culture. This happens because they are seeing the world through the lens of their biblical identity and not merely through a cultural identity. Teaching students to think biblically in the world is one of the most important tasks we have as a YTH leader.

What does that look like?

Students love conversations on purpose and identity.

Cru was originally founded as Campus Crusade for Christ in 1951 when Bill and Vonette Bright began a student ministry on the UCLA campus in Southern California. God had given them a vision for the total fulfillment of the Great Commission throughout the world. (2) The Cru mentality is one of design and helping young people on the campus know who they are. I reference them here because they have a distinct mission to help young people find their place in the world.

In a recent article on the Cru website blog, identity is defined this way:

> "Over the course of our lives, each person's identity is being formed and shaped through individual experiences, relationships, culture, media and the world around us. We are constantly seeking to define who we are in any way that we can. We may receive an overwhelming amount of messages telling us to define ourselves by external measures, but what would it look like to base our identity on the way God sees us?"

Basing our identity on the way God sees us is brilliant. Here are a few quick references we should be teaching our YTH about how God sees them:

Ephesians 1.18
"I pray that the eyes of your heart may be enlightened in order that you may know the hope to which he has called you, the riches of his glorious inheritance in his holy people..."

There is so much more in Ephesians 1, but, the idea is to ask ourselves how does God see us? Maybe one of the best identity chapters in the Bible is found in this chapter. Paul is addressing the church in Ephesus, and as he does, he begins to explain a new way of thinking. A new identity for believers. Paul begins by praying we would have our eyes opened to the hope God has called us to. Wow. I love that. This is great news for every teenager.

Then Paul says if we are in Christ, then we should, according to Ephesians 1, be *blessed* with every spiritual blessing; and we have been *chosen, adopted, redeemed, forgiven, grace-filled,* and *unconditionally loved* and *accepted*. It goes on to say that we are *pure, blameless,* and *forgiven*. Finally, that we will receive the *hope* of spending eternity with God in heaven. I think hope is one of the most attractive traits we should be teaching our young people. Whoa, what a definition of identity.

A proper purpose and spiritual identity for teenagers is really simple:

Once you have committed your life to Christ, you now define your life by what the Word or scripture says about you, not by what the world or culture says about you. You are now chosen, adopted, redeemed, forgiven, grace-filled, and unconditionally loved and accepted.

Paul also said in 2 Corinthians 5 that old things have passed away and new things have come to our life when we are in Christ. A true understanding of Christianity is transformation that looks like "we once were, but now we are." We used to be one way, but now we are another way. No matter what the world says about me and its cultural morality, what matters most is what God says about me and my biblical morality.

With this biblical identity in mind, the same kind of framework can be used in the adolescent development of their sexual identity.

The Sexual Revolution (Purity as identity)
*This will be itemized and dealt with in more detail in the following book on YTH & Sexuality, but, let's highlight a biblical framework in scripture that will lead you to a simple sexuality ethic.

There have been several Sexual Revolutions in America. But it is undeniable YTH ministry is presently being done in the middle of another *Sexual Revolution* in America. However, this revolution may be the most graphic and redefining *Sexual Revolution* we have seen. A YTH ministry that does not address this *Sexual Revolution* will be a YTH ministry out of context – out of touch with teens today.

A Sexual Revolution includes hot button topics such as redefining marriage, the women's equality movement, sanctity of life, changing boundaries of sexual behavior, censorship in the media, gender identity confusion, and the gay movement as broad as LGBTQ+. What happens in a revolution is the challenging of standardization. No doubt this is happening in the arena of sexuality in our society today.

> *This present Sexual Revolution is challenging society by pressing the envelope of thought while void of a biblical identity and purpose. It is a Revolution whose thinking is void of truth because it is based upon a shifting cultural milieu, rather than thinking that is vetted in truth because it is based in a scriptural framework.*

Personal Ethic of Sexuality

Getting to your personal ethic of human sexuality requires thought discipline. By removing what culture says or what our feelings are about a topic, we then can look at a biblical standard of creation intent in human sexuality fashioned by our creator in scripture. Standardization. Now, there's a word that does not go well in our culture today.

Standardization is a common word for non-negotiables or absolutes or essential features of something. The problem is that when most people think about moral standards, they become situational in their ethic and form their opinion or belief from cultural or personal morality rather than biblical morality. I understand not everyone derives their morality from the bible – and I also understand those who do, do not always come out thinking the same way.

Personally, I have derived my sexuality ethic from the bible and that forms my theology of sexuality.

It is undeniable YTH Ministry is presently being done in the middle of another *Sexual Revolution* in America. A YTH ministry that does not address this *Sexual Revolution* will be a YTH ministry out of context – out of touch with teens today.

The Sexual Revolution is a broad movement that encompasses many topics and issues which necessitates YTH ministry to create an ethic of biblical sexuality. Here is how I have processed my theological ethic of sexuality:

1. Our personal sexuality belief will come from culture or from scripture. It is our personal ideological (cultural) or our theological (biblical) framework.
2. It will be changing if it comes from an ideological or cultural framework, but, it will be constant if it comes from a scriptural framework. That explains why in the past 25 years the sexual revolution has been pressed and changed from a more conservative to a more progressive stance.
3. I know we look at and interpret scripture differently. But there are enough clear guidelines in scripture to agree on when other texts may not seem clear to both sides.
4. There are constants in human sexuality theology - Genesis 1-3, Matthew 5, 15, and 19, Romans 1, and 1 Corinthians 6 are just a few very clear theological foundations of human sexuality. These are the words of Moses, Jesus, and Paul.

5. In these texts, Moses, Jesus, and Paul did have something to say about human sexuality. Definitions or prohibitions related to gender, marriage, sexual immorality (adultery, fornication, homosexuality, prostitution, idolatry, abnormality, incest, and beastiality) even if they did not directly address the specific word of the topic in question.

6. What we do know conclusively from these texts, is that each author kept marriage and sexual relations inside of the marriage union between a man and a woman. It is also conclusive in these texts that God created two binary genders in the human species – male and female as the persons set apart for the sacredness of humanity and marriage.

7. There are many other verses inspired by the Holy Spirit on this topic including Galatians 5, 1 Timothy 1, and Revelation 18, 21. All of these author's words have these original texts from Moses as foundational unity on their stance on the subject.

8. Any deviation from the biblical form or ethic was not the creation intent of Moses' description or Jesus' stance or Paul's address of the human sexuality topic. Any deviation then becomes a secondary un-natural order; a cultural or personal order and not a scriptural order or ethic.

9. Where our sexuality experiences from culture or from personal ideology are in disharmony with these foundational texts in scripture, we must either receive *deliverance* from God, or, develop *discipline* within ourselves from the temptations. Some things we are *delivered* from and some things we are *disciplined* from.

10. In any case, or whether the theological side we may be on, what must be concluded by all is that our differences should not divide us.

If we have a different interpretation of human sexuality in the scriptures than some people may have, it doesn't change our relationship with them. Maybe you believe, as I have stated, that marriage is between a man and a woman, that sex before marriage, outside of marriage, or with the same sex is un-natural and outside of God's intent, and that God created humanity male and female. But do not let this change our relationship with people.

> *So, can a person who breaks one of these prohibitions inherit salvation and heaven? Of course. Any scriptural order or prohibition about gossip, lying, stealing, or sexual sin is forgiven when we ask for God's grace (by faith) and cease from the behavior or practice (by works). If an order or prohibition is practiced under deception and not disobedience I believe it will be up to God to answer this question personally.*

Again, this topic will be itemized and dealt with in complete detail in the following book on YTH & Sexuality. This section is meant to give you a basic structure of cultural and scriptural components to do the work yourself in this area. I am in the midst of a thorough work to be published in 2020 dealing with all sides of the Sexual Revolution in a comprehensive book.

Here's another trend I see in YTH ministry in America.

Worship Movement

One of the most encouraging trends happening across our nation is the rise in worship (musical) and the emphasis upon presence in YTH ministry. To be honest, this really should be an easy shift for YTH leaders. Because our students love music.

> *We don't have to teach students how to worship. They already worship stuff, icons, materialism, others, and self. No, we don't need to teach teens how to worship. What we need to do is teach teens how to worship God.*

The strength of worship in a generation is really about idolatry - removing anything that is placed before God. Whether we are talking about Hollywood, athletes, the sexual revolution, social media, or meism and the idol of self, today's teens are being raised in a sensual culture that has added to their idolatry. All we need to do is to replace this idol worship with the worship of Christ and we will see spiritual formation in teenager's lives and in the culture of the YTH ministry at a rapid pace.

Listen, music is at the core of a teenager's being.

They cannot escape it. Teenagers hear music in the car, music on their phone, music on the television, music in the theaters, music at their sporting events, and music at the mall. The musical worship and response to Christ is innate in young people. It's no wonder or surprise we see a growing emphasis of worship and presence in YTH ministry. Just read the worship scenes of heaven in The Revelation. Pretty spectacular and supernatural.

As YTH leaders we must place a greater focus on increasing the opportunities for our students to worship in the YTH group setting and in their personal lives. Even if we may not have the resources. That is something we will address further later on in the book.

The Mystical Teenager

The mystical and supernatural teenager is alive and well on the planet.

Teens are being raised in a mystical and supernatural culture and because of this, we are seeing a growing worship emphasis in the YTH ministry of the church create a presence-based ministry like we saw decades ago. One of the ways this can be seen is in the rise of the number of elite worship teams and bands and movements that have captured the imagination and the fascination of teenagers in a music driven world. This global worship movement has piqued the interest of a generation.

In light of this movement, many YTH ministries are shifting from a solely program-based or small group (non-YTH service) setting to a presence-based experiential setting. Again, this is not to say a complete departure from small groups is happening, but, a greater emphasis upon worship and presence in various forms is becoming popular.

This switch to a presence-based worship model from the program-based small group model is being done in many settings and in varying degrees and for varying reasons. It may not be a total switch at the YTH service level, but, it is increasing in importance.

This switch is happening because of several reasons:

- I think the main reason for the shift is the hunger of teenagers and their natural generational trait and affinity to the supernatural – and how worship fits into that desire
- The focus on worship from global worship movements has become viral in social media, YouTube, Spotify, and other platforms
- The delay of this shift to a presence-based model in many YTH ministry settings was a result of a YTH leader's lack of a vision for worship – and that vision is changing
- A weakness in the YTH ministry's musicianship could be the reason a YTH ministry has not made the switch. And to be honest, these last two bullets are interrelated.

Because if there is no vision for worship in the YTH ministry, it will not attract musicians.

- Another force in this shift is the overall church growth in its worship environment. This has forced the YTH ministry to grow in the experiential setting also.
- One of the other reasons for this growth is the ease of use with worship through playlists on music player apps and YouTube
- In my conversations with YTH leaders, one of the key reasons for the shift is that the small group setting too often lacks the presence of God and the moving of the Spirit and His gifts. And we cannot lose this in YTH ministry.

This has created a good change for young mystics. Understand, it's not that small groups are being canceled completely. Just that they are not the sole focus of our discipleship or our YTH ministry emphasis. Presence has become a growing and important focus of our discipleship.

Discipleship in Worship

There was a steep rise in the value of small group in the past 15 years. This came about from conferences that boasted how small group was the best format for discipleship. And it became popular to blame the large group worship setting as the cause for a lack of discipleship and spiritual maturity in teenagers. I couldn't disagree more.

Trust me, it's not that I am down on small groups. I've done small group discipleship in YTH ministry 36 years ago. But the small group setting was not the only point of my discipleship. We had a more holistic approach that included presence-based preaching and teaching in the *large group* setting to create discipleship and spiritual maturity in our teenagers. That included prayer and response time after messaging so students could respond to the series we were preaching or teaching on. Our approach also included a fine-tuned *small group* setting for discipleship.

> *A disciplined homiletic and worship setting is not a discipleship weakness nor does it lack the presence of God. In fact, it is just the opposite. A disciplined homiletic and worship setting can quicken the spiritual maturity in teenagers by connecting teens with prophetic theology and mystical worship – the supernatural trait born in Gen Z.*

I have had the conversations with YTH leaders who insist that preaching is not one of their main tasks in ministry. I have heard them say they focus on relationships, events, programming, and discipleship in the small group setting. Again, please do not hear my lack of recognition or respect for the use of small groups.

But, maybe the reason for some of the YTH ministry struggle and the 4% worldview among Gen Z is that the small group model is not working. This is why I believe an increase in our YTH preaching and worship can become revelatory in its function.

Mini-Movements

Listen to what George Barna, the founder of Barna Research, said about the growth of alternative faith-based ministry in relation to the local church. A growth he demonstrates will move from 5% of Americans involvement in 2000 to 35% in 2025 as their primary means of spiritual experience:

"How is it that mini-movements (faith-based, outside the church moments) have fostered impressive life-changes when many local churches have failed to produce similar outcomes? An observation is that each of the mini-movements establishes a place in a person's life through a very narrow focus – prayer, worship, worldview, musical expression, or whatever." (2)

> *What Barna was introducing – 15 years ago – was the importance of the momentary sudden spiritual transformation that comes in experiential settings. The research is showing far too often these moments are not happening in the church. They are happening in a camp, convention, retreat, outreach, or other para-church setting. That is a missed opportunity for the church.*

A very narrow focus – prayer, worship, worldview (theology), or musical expression. Perfectly said in my opinion.

Could it be the church has spent too much time programming? Has YTH ministry over-emphasized programming over presence?

Again, this is not a call for the removal of programming or small group from our ministry. But it is evident in my travels, and, it is evident in the research, that the church needs more interruptions. It is very difficult to set an atmosphere of God's presence and have a time of response in our streamlined 75 minutes we cram full of elements such as starting late, wasted time, announcements, games, small group, a sermonette, little prayer time, and little worship or response times.

When it comes to worship, I am watching the mystical and supernatural trait of young people heightened by an emphasis of worship in the YTH setting. Teenagers already have a fascination with music and ambience. Through this growing worship movement the Holy Spirit has become resident in YTH groups across our nation. Preaching and worship go together and create a magnetic setting charged with the presence of God.

Again, it really is not difficult to get teenagers to worship God because worship is already a part of their lives. What happens when we get our students into His presence is God can do more in a moment than in hours of our own efforts.

The Arts as Discipleship

One of the great ways to do discipleship with teenagers is to appeal to their gifts and talents. If we are not planning for the use of student gifts and talents in the YTH worship setting, we are missing a major proponent of engaging our teenagers in YTH ministry and discipleship.

What are we talking about?

It could be their musical, technology, communication, thespian, organizational, or spiritual skills. The student use of their gifts is a vital part of their faith development and formation. One of the great ways to do this is to involve students in the YTH ministry by using their gifts and talents.

The fine arts gifts and talents of students is at an all-time high. Maybe this is being helped because of competition shows like *Idol* or *Dancing with the Stars*, or *America's Got Talent*. The arts in the form of musical worship, poems and spoken words, drama, short story, or artistic expressions have added to the mystical or spiritual part of the culture of YTH. Maybe it is the use of a student's organizational skills in the administration of the YTH ministry, or, the spiritual gifts of prayer that will bring ownership and involvement in the YTH ministry.

Some students have leadership abilities that could add to the biblical, theological, and discipleship part of YTH ministry also. No matter the gift, in any case, we must free our students to participate actively in their YTH group. Watching teens use their gifts in the YTH ministry setting is both inspirational (mystical) and biblical (ethical).

Let me add one more reason for highlighting this growing worship movement in our YTH groups.

A Student's School Format

This has been addressed briefly earlier in the book and is something that is really important to consider.

The reality that students are already in a small group classroom setting 35 hours a week in school should cause us to ask if it is best to put the students back into this setting again in YTH ministry every week. Students run from classroom to classroom all week and are sitting in front of a teacher listening to a lecture most of the week. They are being taught so much about the world around them all week at school. How much have they experienced and learned about God and theology when they are at home or church?

We have already begun to see in the stats pouring in on the last two generations that maybe poorly run graded age-stage small groups are not the best way for us to do theology and discipleship. The best format for teenagers to be discipled in YTH ministry is an experiential kinesthetic relationship with God. It is in this setting that discipleship and spiritual formation come alive in a dynamic way.

If our students are not in a presence-based YTH ministry setting, complete with theological preaching and a worship ethic that includes the operation of the gifts and time for a student response, then they are missing a large part of theology – of finding out who God is through an experiential approach. A balance of these is best. Ask yourself this question.

Do your students get the chance to worship God in the YTH setting? I'm talking about the moving of the Spirit through corporate worship and the operation of the gifts of the Spirit and allowing space and time for students to respond to God. One of the purest ways we can introduce God to this generation is in our response to His presence through worship.

My YTH group today has a healthy balance of this.

A typical YTH service setting will have the pre-event relationship building time for social relations. We then go into the large room and worship for 20 minutes or more. This is our time to express our relationship to God and for ministry to take place. This is most often proceeded by prayer time and then into the ministry of the word. When this is complete, the students and leaders dismiss into a response to the message that might be on their own or into their small groups to talk it out and to pray with each other. Most of the time, after this, we finish the evening in worship and music together again.

The strength of our approach is the leadership development and shared ownership of both students and adult leaders in the entire setting. In the coming days, it will be important to make sure your students are getting a chance to respond to God in the YTH setting. More on that shortly.

Let me cover this last trend.

A Diversity Movement

A trend in diversity? This isn't something most adults would admit.

Just listening to the news and the proliferation of racism and violence and anger, you would think that diversity would NOT be a significant trend in our YTH culture and much less the church. But, be careful to who you are listening to. Because it is undeniable that one of the growing traits of this generation has become an emerging force in our culture today.

That movement is diversity.

With the prevailing racism and dissension in America, this younger generation is going to have a say in the future landscape of American race relations if we let them. We are seeing a reconciliation and healing and inclusion narrative in young people all across the country. I believe if we put the pen in the hand of this generation they will finish the narrative of Martin Luther King, Jr. when he cried,

*"I have a dream that **one day** little black boys and black girls will be able to hold hands with little white boys and white girls as sisters and brothers...and join hands and sing in the old Negro spiritual, 'free at last, free at last, great God almighty we are free at last.'"*

"One Day". It is closer to that day than yesterday.

Please hear me. I did not say there isn't racism in America. I think if you reread the last two paragraphs you would see this. But what I did say very clearly is that there is a growing gracism amongst the young people in America. Gracism is not my word.

Gracism

I first heard this concept several years ago reading a book by David Anderson, Lead Pastor of one of America's great inter-cultural churches. In his book called *Gracism: The Art of Inclusion,* pastor Anderson gets into what he calls the answer to racism.

> *On the art of inclusion, Anderson writes, "The parts that we think are less honorable we treat with special honor (taken from I Corinthians 12:23). When people deal with color, class or culture in a negative way that is called racism. But the answer is not to ignore differences as if they don't matter. Instead, we can focus on diversity in a positive way, as an opportunity to show God's favor to everyone. That is gracism. It is when we respond to prejudice and injustice with the principle of radical inclusion for the marginalized and excluded." (3)*

Building on the apostle Paul's exhortations in 1 Corinthians 12 to honor the weaker member, Anderson presents a biblical model for showing special grace to others on the basis of color, class or culture. He offers seven sayings of the *gracist* with practical examples for building bridges and including others in our life. A Christian alternative to secular models of affirmative action or colorblindness, gracism is an opportunity to extend God's grace to people of all backgrounds by valuing their color and race and not pre-judging them.

This is what we are seeing in Gen Z!

In the Barna 360 study of February 2018, Gen Z was found to be the most diverse generation in American history. (4) The statistic shows that 80% of the Millennial and the Gen Z set have persons of the opposite race in their circle. We cannot silence their growing voice on this topic but we must celebrate it so they can write the next national narrative in America. I see this growing gracism everywhere in our YTH culture!

Gracism is not just about the ETHNIC part of the problem. It is about the ETHICAL part of the problem as well.

Watching YTH ministry across America with its broad diversity and inclusion is very encouraging. I truly believe YTH ministry today in the Millennial and the Gen Z set has the solution to the problems we are facing. Wouldn't it be refreshing to see a panel of students interviewed by the media and to hear their stories of inclusion and respect and love? The way I have watched young people work together could be a wind of reconciliation to our nation.

There are so many settings in our country where *gracism* is exercised over *racism*. Where *unity* is more important than *punity*. Where *love* is more practiced than *hatred*. I do not believe people are born racist. As a matter of fact, when you see the younger generation and how they exercise play, neighborhood relationships, athletic team participation, working jobs together, social posting of inter-cultural relationships, and honor among race, you have to wonder when does racism begin? And who is teaching our young people to hate?

> *If the media and the angry adults in our nation could visit the younger generation in their pursuit of ethnical unity and ethical valuation of each other nation-wide, they would be encouraged. It is a message of diversity and a movement we must allow to be celebrated so that it can silence the sins of our past. It is a narrative being written. Even if at an alarmingly slow rate compared to the hate and racism that is being told in ever-increasing waves.*

Please hear me. I did not say racism in America does not exist. What I am saying is that gracism is growing up right alongside of it but we haven't recognized it yet.

"Tell Me Who You Are"

Here is another case in point.

I came across this amazing work from two teenagers, Winona Guo and Priya Vulchi, who are trying to do something about ethnic inequality and diversity development in their peers and specifically in the school setting. It is the cause and passion from students like this around the country who have me so hopeful. In their recent book, *Tell Me Who You Are,* they give 10 concrete steps for how to share your personal story with another person and how to converse with others to know their story.

Hear about this project in their own words.

> *"And we also talk about how the goal here is not to grab the nearest person of color and force them to talk about race. It's about equipping yourselves first with racial literacy in order to be able to apply that lens to every part of your life [and] doing the work first. [It's] about self-activating before you can show up as an activist for others."* (5)

It is these kind of voices we must listen to. We have to give the pen to this generation and let them re-write the narrative. Instead of copying and pasting the old narrative. If we celebrate the gracism of a healing nation, instead of celebrating the racism of a broken nation, we will get to where we want to be much quicker. Especially if people of privilege make it easier.

"One Day"

Maybe you've heard the term *microaggressions.* These are unconscious or hidden expressions people have about race or prejudice. Because these exist in all of us, we can never stop apologizing. All of us can delay the *One Day* if we fail to model to the next generation how to walk hand in hand and live in awareness and apology for our privilege.

At some point in time our elders in the civil rights and race relations arena must promote the powerful healing taking place and not squelch it with continued promotion of the past. We must step up as YTH leaders and promote our children and their beautiful story of inclusion, healing, and gracism. The young people I speak with weekly across our country are perfect examples of this and they want to be heard.

I cannot tell you how many times I've heard a teenager say to me they love their brother or sister of color. I cannot tell you how often I see people of color as best friends, or on the same athletic team, or studying together, or sitting next to each other in the YTH service, or sitting on the floor praying together. They are modeling the answer in front of a world that simply will not see this growing trend or listen to their new story.

"One Day" we must listen to the voices of our young people.

All throughout history God has had young biblical justice and culture producers. **Moses** grew up in an intercultural setting that has destroyed lesser people. **Esther** wasn't afraid of someone who wanted to kill her race off and she spoke to a King to save her people. **Daniel** wasn't afraid of the king of Persia or the nations that were judging him for being a follower of Jehovah. **Paul** wasn't afraid of the Roman Empire to speak to both Jews and Gentiles. Even **Jesus**, as middle-eastern was used to break the dividing wall down in Jerusalem as a remarkable leader against the religious and pagan system of Rome that included multiple ethnicities.

Throughout history black and white people such as Abraham Lincoln (in later life), William Wilberforce, Susan B. Anthony, Harriet Tubman, Frederick Douglass, Lena Horne, Whitney Young, Jr., Muhammed Ali, Rosa Parks, William Moore, Billy Graham, Dietrich Bonhoeffer, Joan Trumpauer, Aretha Franklin, Coach Tony Dungy, Oprah Winfrey, and Scott Hagan would all make their mark on equality and justice. We cannot let their work be in vain. The work of these crucial black and white activists has set the stage for where we are today.

I could name other contemporaries I respect greatly in this movement you would not know. What must be clear though, is that we must continue to celebrate and promote the greater narrative of gracism spreading in our young people today. The work this younger generation is experiencing because of the forefathers of justice movements before us. If we fail to tell this new story our young people are writing for us, we are turning our back on those who have sown and worked for this moment.

I think today can be our *"One Day"*.

It is time we honor these great civil rights and social justice leaders by our dedication to speed up the age-out narrative and make racism more of a reminder of how things used to be rather than re-introducing it to a generation who does not want to repeat the sins of our fathers. How long are we going to let the privileged narrative of racism in our country re-educate our children? We derive our own personal dedication to social justice from the many voices who have stood and cried out in our history for healing.

I believe all across our nation – and the world for that matter – this new generation is quietly refreshing the story. If we are willing to read their story and help publish it for them our *"One Day"* could be today.

We must let them be the answer to Dr. King's speech, that *"One Day"* is today.

I've seen the *"One Day"* in 2019 in California, New Jersey, Wisconsin, Missouri, Belgium, Florida, Oregon, Nebraska, and Kentucky. I've seen it in Sydney, Pennsylvania, Arizona, Colorado, Texas, and Indiana. This is not anecdotal. I've seen it in South Dakota, Michigan, and Illinois. I've seen it in the rural, the suburban, and the urban setting among middle school students and high school students. This is a statistical data fact happening right before our eyes as the most diverse generation in history is speaking loud and clear.

> *I believe it is happening because of many of my hard working and dedicated black friends who have humbly kept the message of healing before us. I know them personally. I speak with them regularly. And I need to encourage them to continue because their message is working. Their message of healing is being born in the children and teenagers of our nation!*

Privilege

A white friend of mine said one time, "How long do we have to apologize?" After stopping my eyes from rolling and calming down, I simply responded, "Until we're dead." And I meant it. I know there is a deeper thought in that question, but, the simplest answer is that by apologizing we are modeling the language and behavior for a new generation. It is equally important for those who apologize for racial prejudice that those who have been hurt will accept the apology. Everyone must live an apologetic life in regard to the feelings of others every day.

People who weren't hurt do not control when people who were hurt will heal and move on.

Let's deal with this sin of partiality quickly so we can change our perspective and help this wave of gracism continue to grow.

What has been called "psychological wage" or "invisible backpacks" or "implicit bias" or "critical race theory" will all help us define race privilege. Using these terms as a conglomerate definition, privilege is the advantage, perceived or real, of a race in their dominant setting (nation, region, or neighborhood). It can be further understood by looking at *white* privilege in America, *black* privilege in Africa, *Asian* privilege in the Orient, or *brown* privilege in Latin settings (nation, region, or neighborhoods).

Every group must face their privilege and how they relate to the minority in their setting. It is broadly true that white, black, brown, and all others must work together shedding privilege in whatever setting we are dominant. But, what is most prevalent in this section of the writing is this overwhelming concept concerning the white privilege in most parts of America.

I know white privilege created the history of racism and prejudice in our nation. I know history is still being repeated by too many. Our white privilege is arrogant and sinful. That is clear and without argument. In this moment of the book I want to bring a challenge to every race of privilege in their dominant setting:

Shed with humility and intention the advantage, specialness, or immunity that we enjoy over the other groups in our setting.

Because, as James, the brother of Jesus has said, we must "Avoid the evil of partiality." (James 2.1-4)

The best way to do this is to begin with our young people. We cannot retrain this present younger generation to hate each other. As a people in America today, we must listen to the younger generation and their narrative of inclusion, diversity, and gracism. If we see clearly, we will recognize the growing gracism and acceptance and healing and inter-racial relationships that are being built right before our eyes in our young people.

I Have A Dream

As we have said, the Millennial and the Gen Z sets are the most diverse generational group in American history. If we allow, this could be the most important generational narrative in the long history of racism in our nation – that a generation will use their characteristic trait to put an end to racism everywhere.

We are going to get what we celebrate.

Why not take the small steps to celebrate the beautiful diversity of our young people and teenagers? Why not become the fulfillment to Dr. Martin Luther King, Jr's *I Have A Dream* speech and allow this present day generation to be the "*One Day*"? I'm not talking about the denial of a problem. I'm talking about the declaration of an answer. I believe the young people in America hold the answer in their heart and with their hands as they embrace each other with their God-given love.

We can do this best by letting Martin Luther King, Jr's prayer ring true today in our children:

"I have a dream that my four little children will one day live in a nation where they will not be judged by the color of their skin but by the content of their character. I have a dream that one day little black boys and black girls will be holding hands with little white boys and white girls as sisters and brothers…and join hands and sing in the old Negro spiritual, 'free at last, free at last, great God almighty we are free at last.'"

Thank you Mr. King. Thank you. Because I see that dream coming true Mr. King. Right before our eyes. If only we could all see it like you did.

Action Steps

Family

- *We need a renewed dedication to family devotions at home – whether around the dinner table or in the kids bedroom before they go to sleep, or at the kitchen table before school*
- *Annual meetings with parents of teens to inform, train, and build relationships between the home and the church*
- *Using student homes as small groups, events venues, or meeting places throughout the region for the YTH ministry*
- *Are you involving parents of teens on the leadership team?*
- *Talk about how to model a healthy YTH leader home*

Theology

- *Theology must be a part of the YTH leaders life: set aside 2 hours of bible study or reading each week, sit with an elder in theology once a month, take an online theology course and have the church pay for it*
- *One of the ways to challenge young people in theology is to include the following theological content: the 10 Commandments, key Old Testament Bible stories, the New Testament sermon on the mount of Jesus, the gifts and fruit of the Spirit, key gospel stories, a clear apologetics, and end-time apocalyptic order*
- *Small groups should be a place where students are allowed to ask tough questions and dialogue to increase their biblical framework. Small groups must get beyond just being relational settings and they must challenge the faith of the students in attendance.*
- *Are you expecting and challenging students to bring their Bibles or at least have a Bible app when they come to the YTH service?*

Sexual Revolution

- *The beginning point for dealing with the sexual revolution starts with a spiritual identity ethic and helping students understand their Godly design. Creating series' annually on spiritual identity can become a pro-active response to The Sexual Revolution.*
- *There must be a greater understanding of biblical sexuality in YTH leadership. This includes both the creation intent in Genesis and the messianic intent in Matthew.*

- *Talk about how the YTH ministry culture is modeling a biblically healthy sexuality ethic to teenagers*
- *Do you expect teenagers to behave before they belong? Grace, acceptance, and inclusion must be the approach toward teenagers who are struggling with their sexual identity.*
- *Bring in a therapy/counselor once a year to do a one day seminar on sexuality*

Worship
- *YTH ministry must create periodic nights of worship to assure that students are in a presence based setting with no restrictions. These 'nights of worship' can become an appeal to the mystic and supernatural traits of young people. This will also create teaching settings with no time restraints to take the lids off student worship.*
- *Do a series annually to teach on worship and bring more horizon and practical help to teenagers on how to worship. This can remove lids and time constraints and allow for students to grow in their worship discipline.*
- *With simple bumpers, trailers, and YouTube video assist YTH ministry can add A/V excellence to the setting where a YTH group may not have good musicianship*
- *Tactile worship is a great way to involve worship stations like a sand table, dry erase board, and journaling or writing assignments to increase the worship experience*

Diversity
- *YTH leadership must create diverse teams. We cannot just talk about diversity without modeling diversity in adult, student, host, and worship team involvement.*
- *Be versed on the history of the social justice and civil rights movements*
- *There must be an intentional effort to build relationships in communities of color through external programming*
- *The YTH setting must build avenues of entrance externally and not simply expect people of color to show up to the church. We can prove our diversity ethic with neutral site extension.*
- *Sharing ministry with people of color will bring a Diversity valuation to the overall YTH ministry. Inviting people of color to be guest speakers to the leadership setting or the YTH service.*

"In six weeks over 1,000 young people
were called into ministry and gave their lives
for service to the kingdom"
-Historian of the Asbury College Revival in Kentucky 1970

Chapter 5

The Third (Next) Great Awakening

It is not time for one person to stand in a generation. It is time for an entire generation to stand as one.

America needs another spiritual interruption. This is an important moment in the history of YTH ministry. God gave me an idea 7 years ago – to believe for an Awakening in the young teenagers of our country. Specifically, that we would raise up 1,000 young people who will fast and pray every Friday at lunch. What better time than *The Teen Decade*?

As we said at the beginning of this book, *The Teen Decade* only happens once in a century and it only lasts 7 years. As I finish this book it is 7 years in the writing. I began writing it in 2012. So many prayers. So many messages. And so many conversations with thousands of teenagers and leaders about their place in the world and how they will lead *The Third (Next) Great Awakening*.

I feel like a madman. Repeating myself over and over the last decade trying to get teenagers to see their place in the world and church history. For seven years believing the same thing every day. Before I would go to bed every night I would pray believing the same thing for seven years. When I got up every morning it has been the first thought on my mind for seven years. Now hopefully these words will inspire you to believe with me for the same thing the next seven years.

> *For seven years I have been asking God for a thousand personal revivals and for a thousand teenagers to pray and fast on Fridays. A thousand teenagers who will spark The Next Great Awakening. And at the end of the writing of this book we have just passed over the 1,000 mark in the Fall of 2019!*

Every Friday there are more than 1,000 young people asking God for an Awakening. Would you join us? All you need to do is send me a DM or an email. You will find those details on the website ythology.com.

At this time in a teenager's life they are an empty page waiting for words to be written on. It is in this moment they will make decisions that will help them to find their identity as a human being. It is in this moment they will develop the interests from the setting around them that will lead them to their purpose in life. It is in this moment of their life they will be educated and will shape the way they think. It is in this moment they will have the greatest opportunity to choose their circle of friends who will influence the rest of their lives. This moment may be the critical generational shift our nation needs.

Tipping Points & Violent Success

Malcolm Gladwell wrote a book called *The Tipping Point.* In this book he described the moments where all of the work preceding a moment is actually a catalyst for the moment itself. It is like walking up one side of a teeter totter and coming to the fulcrum in the center. The next step becomes easier as you begin to walk down the other side. The point where momentum makes everything easier.

Gladwell uses a term called the Power of Context. He explains the importance of setting to determine whether a phenomenon could go viral or become populous. Throughout the book, context becomes the place where even small variations in social groups or minor changes in a neighborhood or community take an idea to violent success. (1)

Violent success. I love this concept because it brings tension into the room. And sometimes tension brings change. We could use some more tension and persistent violence in the sense that we cannot give up on the emphasis of the steps it takes to bring revival in the church and awakening in the culture. I believe every organization has tipping points resulting from persistent violence. Many relationships and families have tipping points. Athletic teams have a tipping point in the middle of a game when all of the sudden the momentum changes their way. We can see tipping points throughout the Bible. I'll mention those in a moment.

But it is important to think about this concept as we close out *The Teen Decade.* Could we be in a tipping point moment in YTH ministry? Could it be we are about to hit the fulcrum in the middle and our next steps in YTH ministry could be much simpler than the last steps? Do you think all of the prayers that have been prayed over our nation might finally be coming to a point of the climb where we have reached the tipping point and God does the rest?

As John said in Revelation 8, when the bowl is full, the Angel pours it out onto the earth.

> *I sat down and estimated over 36 years of YTH ministry, not to mention my personal times of prayer, I have been in around 5,600 corporate prayer meetings (church, YTH group, camp, conventions, retreats, See You At The Pole, and YTH group prayer meetings). That is about an average of 3 corporate prayer meetings a week.*

So many prayers have been prayed for this generation to be awakened. I've been in prayer meetings with students and leaders the past seven years and have seen and heard it all:

- I've watched students and leaders weep before God in repentance of their sin
- We've toured around the world with a globe or a map in global prayer for the greatest spiritual move of God in our nation's history
- I've watched students in small groups at the front of YTH service with clenched fists praying together for their families
- We have prayed in schools and around flag poles in the rain, snow, and heat for their friends, teachers, and coaches
- Students have sent me DM's with photos of them praying in the lunch room and reading their bibles in front of their friends
- I've been in inter-denominational campus clubs like FCA, Young Life, and First Priority praying in the classroom or the choir room
- A group of students from a campus club stood with me at Stoneman-Douglas HS and we prayed for the school, the community, and our nation after the shooting
- In so many camps, conventions, and YTH retreat weekends I've been with students and leaders crying out to God for revival in America
- I've been in city-wide prayer concerts with thousands of inter-denominational friends where students and leaders have been on their face asking God for the greatest Awakening in our nation's history
- We have packed homes with small groups where students were lying on the floor in a leaders home with 15 students worshipping and interceding
- One of my favorite memories in prayer is riding through our community in a van or a bus on 'prayer drives'

- Walking the school campus with students and laying hands on the buildings and praying for the staff, faculty, and students

I've seen it with my own eyes. They really believe it.

> *Do you think those prayers have gone unheard? Do you think God has turned His back on all of those prayers? Do you think Jesus is wearied by a generation's prayers? Do you think the Holy Spirit is unable to answer each of those prayers? I don't believe so. As a matter fact, I believe the sacrifices and the prayers of this generation have caught the attention of God and I believe with everything in me that we are so close to The Third (Next) Great Awakening in America. An undeniable moment.*

SYATP

See You At The Pole (SYATP) was proof God can move in a moment.

The church has a great opportunity before it, but, with that opportunity comes a responsibility to steward the resources available that will give the church a platform to teenagers in their most formative years. I am idealistic enough to believe one good idea can last a long time. The example of the one junior high school student who wanted to pray around her flagpole in 1990 is still working today 30 years later. Her YTH Pastor and some friends ran with her idea and 30 years later most of you have gathered at flag poles across America for See You At The Pole (SYATP).

It all started with one young girl on a rainy morning in Dallas. There have been many tipping points throughout time that attest to the staying power of a good idea.

SYATP was a tipping point for YTH ministry in the modern era. As you saw in the chapter on the history of YTH ministry, we haven't had enough of those and we need some more moments right now. The students we are working with have the greatest opportunity to see the greatest revival in world history. Why? Because they are living in the worst days it assures God and His mercy is going to be poured out. Sometimes it takes the worst of times to bring about the best of times.

I have been asking for a thousand personal revivals that will change a thousand teenager's lives! Our students will be known for seizing this timely opportunity, or, for snoozing through this important time in history. I believe they are ready and I believe when it happens they will not be surprised because they have asked for this faithfully. So why not a thousand suddenlies interrupting this generation? Sometimes it is suddenlies and tipping points that create the momentum that creates the win.

Like in a flu outbreak or an organizational turnaround.

> *In a tragic way, the flu epidemic in the spring of 1918 on the east coast was begun by WWI sailors visiting Philadelphia for a parade, and 6 months later more than 50 million people were dead worldwide. Because of a cough in a public restaurant or bathroom or on a parade route. Interruptions happen all the time and can become pandemic in months.*
>
> *In a productive way, The Hush Puppies organization was going to close in 1984. A struggling company had only sold 30,000 shoes in its first decade of existence. Fearing closure, the company made a small change in a marketing meeting – place a puppy on the shoes. The next decade they sold 430,000 shoes. The next year, 1996, they sold 2 million pairs of shoes!*

The Bible talks about tipping points and violent success also. There are at least 83 mentions of a suddenly moment. Here are a few:

Joshua 11 – Joshua's army strikes the king of Hazor suddenly
1 Kings 18 – The death of hundreds of false prophets in a 63 word prayer of prophet Elijah
2 Kings 2 – The chariot of God sweeps Elijah away instantly and he is never seen again
Psalms 6 – God promised our enemies would be ashamed suddenly
Proverbs – Destruction comes upon the foolish suddenly
Prophets – Prophesy of sudden doom upon idolatry suddenly and without warning
Ezekiel 37 – The Spirit of the Lord upon a valley of dry bones suddenly became an army
Matthew 28 – Jesus appears after the resurrection suddenly to Mary and Martha
Mark 1 – The Spirit came on Jesus suddenly at His baptism and He began His public ministry
Mark 13 – The Lord's sudden return and the rapture of believers to heaven
Luke 2 – The Angel hosts announcing the birth of the Christ startled the shepherds suddenly

Luke 19 – Zacchaeus was changed in a moment with one act of perfect timing

Acts 2 – The outpouring of the Spirit upon mankind happened suddenly from heaven

Acts 16 – The earthquake opened the prison door for Paul and Silas struck without warning

Acts 9, 22 – The Lord's Light shone on Paul out of nowhere and knocked him to the ground

I believe the reason why some of us never grow up spiritually is because God has left the room and we don't even know it. Eli (1 Samuel 3) and Samson (Judges 16) didn't know the Lord left them and continued on without His presence. God would come again and break the silence when Eli and Sampson would hear God speak in a matter of days after there had been no voice. There are points of absolute change and we need a suddenly again today.

In the scriptures they are called "miracles", "signs and wonders", or "suddenlies". When the Spirit and human effort create divine momentum and irreversible change. It is viral, epidemic, pandemic, contagious, rapid, impulsive, and instant. God wants to awaken you from your sleep and stir you suddenly and maybe even unknowingly.

The Perfect Storm

We could see a perfect storm – the traits of a generation, the condition of society, and the move of God – on this generation. An interruption of epic proportion. What better time? Look at the characteristic traits of this present YTH generation and see how quickly God could move in their lives and in their world.

Generational Traits

One of the most comprehensive studies on the Millennial and the Gen Z sets has been done in the past few years and is helping us know how to approach this generation and how to use these characteristic traits most effectively. The studies have been numerous from Christian Smith (Soul Searching: The Religious and Spiritual Lives of American Teenagers), Pamela Irwin (A Critical Approach to Youth Culture), David Kinnaman (You Lost Me, UN-Christian), James Emery White (Meet Generation Z), and the most recent from Barna called Impact 360 study. Each of these studies have been an exhaustive finding on the details and the characteristic traits of this present generation of young people.

These studies have become the standard for understanding young people today and there are presently more books being written to help us understand and to reach this generation. There is no way to review these works in this chapter, but, here are a few characteristic highlights from these studies to help you understand young people in America.

Of course, we have to be careful of generalizing characteristic traits over a decade of social study and spreading those traits into two social sets. There are some common traits the Millennial and the Gen Z sets share. So keep in mind in some ways they are not much different than each other. And yet, in some ways they are. So I will dare to place this younger generation into a form of understanding knowing they will wiggle right out of it before this book is fully read.

There are so many generational set traits of the millennials and Gen Z that condition them for an historical moment. Here are a few of these key traits I believe make them even more reachable with the gospel by the church in the next 10 years.

1. Supernatural

When you look at the mystery and the wonder in this generation, you begin to see that they are mystics.

Part of this can be seen in their child-likeness and trusting faith that conditions a generation for a move of God. The ability to believe for more and to dream. You cannot define the gospel or this generation without the supernatural. Our Psalm we are using at the end of this book is a commentary on the works and the wonders and the signs of God to a generation. This generation is inundated with movies and media saturated with the supernatural – at present there are no less than 33 movies and television show around the theme of the supernatural.

Child-likeness and faith is the perfect set-up. There is an Interest and a fascination with the supernatural that is childlike in this generation. The simplicity and the wonder and the awe innate in our children is something we cannot lose in society. Too many times I have heard adults scold the adolescent mind-set and bring them "down-to-earth". To call them away from the juvenialization in our society and to hold them back from mystery and the supernatural. It must be understood from Jesus to Bonhoeffer and from Graham to your YTH leadership today, there has been much said about child-LIKENESS that leads to faith and ultimately the miraculous.

It is this supernatural trait at the foundation of the gospel and this generation. What an explosion waiting to happen!

Why is it that everyone who is young wants to be old, and everyone who is old wants to be young again? Maybe it is the affinity for child-LIKENESS and this love of the supernatural we must foster today. Sure, we need more theology and adolescent to adult growth in YTH ministry. But don't throw the baby out with the bath water! I believe this characteristic trait of the supernatural in the adolescent and young adults can be mined with great results.

How does this change the way we do YTH leadership?

Our students must see what they read in scripture come to their culture. We must prove to our young people God moves outside of the church setting. We must capture the faith and the trust in our young people. We can do this in two ways:

First, by believing ourselves as YTH leaders for the supernatural and creating space for signs and wonders and miracles in our meetings. And *second*, we can capture a teenager's child-like faith by teaching them practical theology to use outside of the church setting and in their world. I believe we have failed too often at those two things in YTH ministry.

2. Risk-taking

Another generational trait in teenagers is risk-taking. Risk-taking is the seedbed for a move of the Kingdom of God in a generation.

I've heard some say adventure is not a part of the vocabulary of Gen Z. Some studies place this Gen Z squad in safety mode and Millennials in a more adventurous mode and others will switch them. You know, the 'snowflakes' and the 'safe places' people. This all depends upon whether a teenager has found their "hill" to die on, their t-shirt message to publish. Because when this happens we will see the passion unhindered.

When it comes to crisis and to cause, this generation will die on their "hill". You see, what we are witnessing in them today is risk-assertiveness and not risk-aversion. Let me prove this point. We are seeing risk-taking and assertiveness in their public display of activism in our nation today for the safety of their campus and our country. We are seeing risk-taking and assertiveness in teenagers fighting against human-trafficking or building wells in Africa or taking missions trips to Central America. The risk-taking increases greatly when young people find their "hill". We will deal with the concept of *wild Awakenings* later in the book.

How does this change the way we do YTH leadership?

We must guide them with our wisdom while not hindering them from their passion. We must lead them to see they can have a dream for their life that is bigger than them. I believe helping to cast vision and purpose is one of the great responsibilities of spiritual leadership around young people. Wisdom and passion are not inseparable. You see, assessed risk-taking will increase the success of a cause or project greater than it will decrease it. Something happens in the life of a teenager when an adult believes in them.

Think of the explosive combination of the wisdom of adults and the passionate risk-taking of Gen Z. This could lead us to a civil (i.e., legislative and campus safety) and a religious (i.e., spiritual and church growth) revival. What many are calling, *'The Third (Next) Great Awakening'*.

3. Cause-oriented

This trait is connected to the second trait. What we have learned watching this generation is they will fight for their cause – anti-human trafficking, gun control in schools, and water wells in Africa are just a few. If we are intentional, that cause could be for the Gospel.

This is one of the most evidential traits of Gen Z. To this generation, their "hill" is their cause and it is worth dying for. It is their reason for being, what wakes them up every morning. When people (not just young people) have discovered their "hill", they become world-changers. Because understanding that purpose will result in Gen Z leaving their legacy behind them for generations to see. Whatever that legacy or cause is. Can you imagine if YTH leaders could lead a generation of 2.5 million young people to lay their lives down for the cause of Christ? It would be nation-changing.

I'm not sure we have ever seen the impact of a teenager in this generation completely on fire for God. What would be the impact on our nation and world if we saw that today in the 2.5 million teenagers who call themselves committed Christians?

How does this change the way we do YTH leadership?

We must help this generation to see the Kingdom of God as their "hill". We have to bring the stories of the past to life again. To bring a new vision and dream for their life. Dreams are best shared in the context of people who believe in us and who are willing to help us to completely fulfill our purpose. The context of the Kingdom in relationship with believers is a great place to develop a lofty identity. An identity that places them as the envoys of the Kingdom of God seeking *The Third (Next) Great Awakening*.

Asking a student specific questions like, what do you want to do when you graduate school? Questions like, what brings your greatest satisfaction? I talk weekly to teens who are searching for the 'why'. Why am I here? Why should I get up in the morning? Why do I matter? Identity is one of the greatest ways to bring personal fulfillment and understanding of the Creator's plan for their life. We have to get students talking about their place in history.

Here's another generational trait of Gen Z.

4. Teamwork

I believe teamwork and connection could be the avenue to the next move of God.

Is there a greater moment in communication history than today? Is there a better way to reach the globe than technology and social media? It is like the perfect set-up for a suddenly or a moment. Let me explain this through a couple of moments in the lifetime of the Millennial and the Gen Z sets.

This is never more illustrated than by the 9/11 impact and the economic crash impact in the beginning and the middle of this generation's lifetime. Crisis made the Millennial and the Gen Z a resilient set. The impact of crisis can be seen in other settings as well. We see it in sports teams, work related projects, school homework projects or labs, and even in the growing diversity and gracism in this generation. One of the things crisis will do is galvanize everyone impacted by it and put us on the same team. Who could forget seeing our government standing side by side on the steps of Capitol Hill in unison singing "God Bless America" to the whole world?

This galvanizing teamwork is one of the admirable characteristic traits of the younger generation also.

We have seen this teamwork also in recent history as evidenced by the handful of students who have come front and center as voices of the Stoneman-Douglas H.S. shooting in Parkland, FL.

They have given themselves the hashtag #MarchForOurLives and #NeverAgain and #fixit so they can build solidarity to their cause of nonviolence in schools. Even their social media following and school partnerships across the nation have gone viral. This support is seen in record-breaking posts, follows, likes, and retweets, and unifying school marches and activism, that screams teamwork. This unity has sent their cause public all the way to the White House.

How does this change the way we do YTH leadership?

Student leadership teams are a must for healthy YTH ministry. Doing something as simple as a survey of core competencies in the YTH ministry will help you to find a variety of gifts and talents in your young people. This should be done every year. When a student recognizes their spiritual gifts it creates an identity that brings confidence and helps them find their place. Every YTH ministry should be thinking of the core traits of their students and how they can program to those traits. Can you imagine the kind of things that can be done with the gifts and talents of your students? We cannot miss this important characteristic trait in this generation.

The final generational trait in Gen Z is undeniable.

5. Publishers/Entrepreneurial vision

Similar to Christianity, I believe this publishing spirit is entrepreneurial and apostolic.

The developing world of technology around Gen Z has given them a lean toward creating, publishing, and producing like no other generation:

- It has been shown by many of these sociological studies and these referenced writers above that Gen Z prefers to start a business than work for one
- They are comfortable creating, publishing, and producing with their phones in the palm of their hand
- Whether it is an app for their photos or an app for their videos, Gen Z has grown up as digital creatives
- These tech tools have caused them to be avant-garde when it comes to their pursuits and ideas
- The result of this entrepreneurial spirit has pushed them into the workforce early

According to one strategist, Deep Patel, *"the newly developing high-tech and highly networked world has resulted in an entire generation thinking and acting more entrepreneurially."* (2)

This is just more support that as YTH leaders we have a responsibility to lead this generation in their hopes and dreams. No teenager should ever pass through their teen years and not have a dream. Something bigger than them. It is innate in each of them. We should not quell these dreams but we should create opportunities around the YTH ministry for these dreams to come true. We should become *imagineers* for the teens under our leadership and create a YTH ministry setting that is an incubator for their dreams and vision.

How does this change the way we do YTH leadership?

As a church we must capture this production-minded content-creating mindset for the sake of the Kingdom. Identify your student's core competencies and skillsets and set them to work for the gospel and the Kingdom. Set them in motion for local and global projects they can work on such as feedONE (Convoy of Hope Children's feeding program) and Speed The Light (a global youth missions program), and World Serve (a humanitarian water and well provider). Put together a creative team of teenagers who can help you with messaging and service planning that will ignite their faith when they see their ideas used in front of their peers.

Let them see the examples and the stories of the people who have gone before them who created local and global impact for the Kingdom of God though their work. Mother Teresa, D.L. Moody, Billy Graham, Truett Cathy, and Reinhard Bonnke came from lowly means and opportunity and believed God for local and global mass works.

The Third (Next) Great Awakening

And this leads us to the cry of this book.

Young people today have never seen a spiritual Awakening in America. They have never known the Church to have a voice of national proportions. Millennials and Gen Z today do not have a concept of the place faith and Christianity can play in the affairs of a society. Their older siblings witnessed the Pensacola, FL outpouring and some may have even seen the end of the Charismatic revival. But these were not nation shaking or systemic changes. The last great Awakening that affected America was the Jesus Movement of the 1960's-1970's – seen by their parents and grandparents.

All of this resulting in the teenagers of America today as the only generation living who have never seen a revival shape a nation.

That's not good enough for me and it shouldn't be for you as a YTH leader.

One of the prayers I have prayed through this decade has been, *"God, I promise to bring this generation before you for the greatest Awakening America has ever seen!"* This has been my consistent prayer for many years. I cannot think of a better time to emphasize this spiritual cry for a generation to see their role in spiritual history for America.

As we have seen at the beginning of the book, America has seen probably four spiritual shifts in her history. Let me finish this chapter by recapping those quickly.

The 1st and 2nd Great Awakenings

We have detailed these earlier, but, let me remind you of the heritage of our nation and the potential promise of God upon our future.

Legendary movements of the mid 1700's and the mid 1800's with Jonathan Edwards and George Whitefield and Charles Finney and D.L. Moody and others. These two movements shaped not only the church but also society. From the eastern shores of the United States came a wave of prayer and intercession through preachers who called the church and the nation to repentance. It was about 100 years of revival fires.

These two movements shaped our nations infancy by grabbing the attention of every sector of society. So much has been written on the influence of the 1st and 2nd Great Awakenings on the landscape of our nation. But here is one entry:

> *The Great Awakenings were religious revivals in the British American colonies mainly between about 1720 and the '40s and also 1790's to the early 1800's. They were a part of the religious ferment that swept Western Europe in the latter part of the 17th century and early 18th century, and then moved swiftly to American soil. The revival preachers emphasized the 'terrors of the law' to sinners, the unmerited grace of God, and the 'new birth' in Jesus Christ. One of the great figures of the movement was George Whitefield, an Anglican priest who was influenced by John Wesley but was himself a Calvinist. Visiting America in 1739–40, he preached up and down the colonies to vast crowds in open fields, because no Church building would hold the throngs he attracted.*
>
> *In addition to Whitefield, Jonathan Edwards was the great academician and apologist of the Great Awakening. A Congregational pastor at Northampton, Massachusetts, he preached justification by faith alone with remarkable effectiveness. He also attempted to redefine the psychology of religious experience and to help those involved in the revival to discern what were true and false works of the Spirit of God.*
>
> *The Great Awakening stemmed the tide of Enlightenment rationalism among a great many people in the colonies. One of its results was division within*

135

denominations, for some members supported the revival and others rejected it. The revival stimulated the growth of several educational institutions, including Princeton, Brown, and Rutgers universities and Dartmouth College. The increase of dissent from the established Churches during this period led to a broader toleration of religious diversity, and the democratization of the religious experience fed the fervor that resulted in the American Revolution.

The Second Great Awakening that began in New England in the 1790s was generally less emotional than the First Great Awakening. The Second Awakening led to the founding of colleges and seminaries and to the organization of mission societies globally."

What is undeniable is that we need another awakening today in our nation. Because at this moment the spiritual formation of our country is non-existent, the church has lost its voice, and our young people have the fastest growing number of atheists in any generational set in American history. What we need is another one of these spiritual movements like we have seen in the past.

Azusa Street Outpouring

The third impacting religious movement in America was the Azusa Street Revival of the early 1900's with William Seymour, Charles Parham, and others. It started in a classroom of Bethel Bible College in Topeka, KS full of college students who wanted more of God and began praying around the clock. The assignment from their teacher was clear. And it resulted in one of the most important religious movements in American History.

Aside from the diversity message that came from the revival (Seymour was a black preacher and Parham was white), the outpouring shaped the beginnings of several Pentecostal denominations that still exist today (Foursquare, Church of God in Christ, and the Assemblies of God to name a few). As this prayer meeting spread from Topeka, Kansas and then Hot Springs, AR, it ended up in Los Angeles. Here is one account of the beginnings of this movement:

"In October 1900 in Topeka, Kansas, a small band of believers led by Charles Parham started Bethel Bible School. The school 'invited all ministers and Christians who were willing to forsake all, sell what they had, give it away, and enter the school for study and prayer, where all of us together might trust God for food, fuel, rent and clothing.' No one paid tuition or board and they all wanted to be equipped to go to the ends of the earth to preach the gospel of the Kingdom as a witness to every nation. The only textbook was the Bible. Their concerted purpose was to learn the Bible not just in their heads but to have each thing in the Scriptures wrought out in their hearts.

As they searched the scriptures, they came up with one great problem - what about the second chapter of Acts? In December 1900, Parham sent his students at work to diligently search the scriptures for the Biblical evidence of the baptism in the Holy Spirit. They all came back with the same answer - when the baptism in the Holy Spirit came to the early disciples, the indisputable proof on each occasion was that they spoke with other tongues.

Armed with this head knowledge, they now sought to have it worked out in their own hearts. They continued the prayer meeting for two more nights and three days. And eventually the movement ended up travelling to Los Angeles, Ca where the century shaping Azusa Street Revival broke out from about 1906 to about 1915." (3)

The tarrying and commitment to wait upon the Lord is what brought one of the most impacting revivals in American history.

The significance of this movement was so important because it spawned a diversity among believers as the fervor from these meetings spread across the country. Several Pentecostal denominations were birthed – including the Assemblies of God, the International Church of the Foursquare Gospel, and the Church of God in Christ. It has been the beautiful relationship between these churches populated with all races that was sparked by this movement 100 years ago.

The Jesus Movement

The last great spiritual movement in America was undoubtedly The Jesus Movement. We have detailed it in chapter 1 on the history of YTH ministry. But, let me say a few other things about the impact of this phenomenon as we move forward.

In Central California in the late 1960's this movement lasted for about 11 years. But its affects were ongoing for 30 years. Rising from the racial tensions spreading from the south and the Hippie Revolution that broke out in The Haight neighborhood of San Francisco, this counter-cultural wave brought a move of the Holy Spirit like an antithetical wave to the culture and society of Central California and the rest of America. The Jesus Movement brought a message of love and faith to a nation hemorrhaging from hate and prejudice.

It was people such as Martin Luther King, Jr. and Billy Graham and Keith Green and Andre Crouch and Nancy Honeytree and Arthur Blessitt and Greg Laurie who all became the fuel to this movement of young adults that evolved from the inner-city, the beaches, and the universities of Central California and across America in the mid- to late- 1900's to Dallas, Kansas City, Memphis, Chicago, Minneapolis, Detroit, Atlanta and the rest of the U.S. that changed an entire nation.

My Humble Means

I was born on the corner of Haight and Ashbury in San Francisco in 1963 – right before The Jesus Movement became viral in public, and, at the same time of the racial riots in *The Haight*, and, while the Supreme Court was removing official Bible reading and prayer from the public school. It is not lost on me that I was born in the center of these movements where so many emotions were rising to the surface. I believe, like you, we were all born with a Creators design. I believe my design was to counter the rise of secular humanism that began to attack our schools and our young people at the same time I was born.

Many times I have visited my birth home on that corner and walked through *The Haight* praying for another Awakening in our country. I have stood in my old apartment, which has become a business now, and asked God to start another revival. I have walked the neighborhoods around Haight Park at the end of the street and wept for the next great spiritual Awakening to rise in America today in what seem like the same conditions as America in the 1970's.

Given the history of Awakenings in our nation, we are sitting in a moment filled with anticipation for what could be the next great spiritual movement in our country.

We are poised for another spiritual Awakening of these proportions soon. To usher this shift into modern America, I have been asking for 'A Thousand Personal Revivals' that will spark *The Third (Next) Great Awakening*. The American YTH culture is in desperate need for a spiritual renewal. And out of great need can come greater works. This should be one of the most exciting times for the YTH leaders of our country. At a time when the hearts of young people are failing, it is a great time for spiritual revival.

Holy Interruptions
There is a list of prophetic words at the end of the book God has given to me for this generation

Interruptions. None of us particularly like them. We like our lives to be predictable and sterile. In America, we default to cautious and safe. Nothing out of the ordinary. Don't distract me when I'm on the phone or watching the game. And stay out of the kitchen if I am cooking. We take the same roads to work every day and we haven't moved our furniture in the office or at home for years.

> *Anyone who knows me would know I am not predictable. I used to bother my wife with moving furniture, people would come into my office and find I had rearranged it the night before, I rarely go to work the same way, and I might bark at you if you interrupt me during the game. Mystery is part of my daily routine. And it is the same for students in many ways. Unpredictable.*

This mystery and unpredictable lifestyle really is scientific also. Look at this research from Neurobiologist Frances Jensen on the teenage brain.

"Teenagers do have frontal lobes, which are the seat of our executive, adult-like functioning like impulse control, judgment and empathy. But the frontal lobes haven't been connected with fast-acting connections yet. The brain actually connects regions from the back of the brain to the front, so the last place to have these fast-acting connections is the frontal lobe."

Dr. Jensen and many other researchers have proven that what we see in this generation could actually be one of its greatest strengths.

She goes on to say, *"But there is another part of the brain that is fully active in adolescents, and that's the limbic system. And that is the seat of risk, reward, impulsivity, sexual behavior and emotion."* (4)

All this to say that mystery is really a part of the young person's life because you never know what you are going to get from them. Their lives are unpredictable because they are not sure what they really want. This is why a student will excite you one minute and then have you crashing the next because of something they've done. Our role as YTH leaders is to make sure we know how to manage this and not to be dismissive of this innate trait. It would do us all a great assist to understand this and *'roll with it'* as they would say.

Why this discussion of interruptions and mystery?

Because interruptions are the way of the Kingdom and they are contrary to western Christianity. A quick read through the New Testament will show the interruption of Christ into the life of Jerusalem and proclaiming a message that was not in vogue. And proclaiming it out of nowhere.

Jesus would surprise the disciples on several occasions by walking through a wall, or on the water from a distance, and even appearing outside of the tomb, or stepping into their walk down the road. Then, following in His footsteps, the Apostles were called out of impossible situations to serve Jesus. I'm sure the townspeople thought He must have been crazy for thinking He could get anything out of these ruffians. But once they were on board with Him, they entered every city they came to and turned it upside down.

Ex Nihilo and Genesis One

The Holy Spirit is really the great interrupter.

It is time for another great interruption in history. We are standing in a time in our nation that is dark. Similar to the description of the world in the beginning of time in the book of Genesis. In chapter one Moses said the earth was formless and void and darkness covered the face of the deep. There was nothingness. It was empty and meaningless. Until the presence of the Holy Spirit began to appear and move over the landscape and create. Out of nothing. In the Latin sense, Ex nihilo, or, *out of nothing*.

Kind of like today. When you look around at our world there are wars, rumors of wars, pestilence, famine, and a humanism that has not allowed for the God of it all back into human history. We look today much like the condition of the world in Genesis 1. Formless, dark, and void. Yet even in this condition there are signs of the Holy Spirit moving over the face of human history to create out of nothing another great creation.

We need another interruption like these other Great Awakenings earlier in this chapter. Like this one at a college in Kentucky.

Over the years I have been encouraged by the outpouring in early American history on University campuses across our nation. Many schools saw a major revival spread through the east coast. Most of the Ivy League schools were begun as ministry training schools because of so many young people being called to mission and ministry in the revivals of the day. But, more recently, something happened in the Midwest that caught my attention and the attention of others across our nation.

Specifically at Asbury College. Read the following report of what happened just a few years ago in my lifetime.

Asbury College, Wilmore, Kentucky
A revival broke out in Asbury College in Wilmore, Kentucky, on Tuesday, February 3rd, 1970.

> *The regular morning chapel at 10 o'clock saw God move on the students in such a way that many came weeping to the front to kneel in repentance, others giving testimonies of confession of sin, and many stories of brokenness. Lectures were cancelled for the day as the auditorium filled with over 1,000 people. Few left for meals. By midnight over 500 still remained praying and worshiping. Several hundred committed their lives to Christ that day.*
>
> *By 6 a.m. the next morning 75 students were still praying, and through the day the chapel filled again as all lectures were again cancelled for the day. The time was*

filled with praying, singing, confessions and testimonies. In 6 weeks over 1,000 young people were called into ministry and gave their lives for service to the kingdom.

Asbury College had been known through the years for its history of great Awakenings and revivals that really led up to the 1970 breakthrough. On several occasions significant moves of the Holy Spirit swept across the nation from the campus.

Here are a list of the other times when the Holy Spirit seemed to be using this college to wake a nation:

-In **February 1905**, during a blizzard, a prayer meeting in the men's dormitory spilled out to the rest of campus and the town of Wilmore.

-In **February 1908**, revival broke out while someone prayed in chapel; the revival lasted two weeks and was signified by prevailing prayer and intercession.

-In **February 1921** the last service of a planned revival lasted until 6 am, and services were extended for three days.

-In **February 1950** a student testimony led to confessions, victories, and more testimonies. This went on uninterrupted for 118 hours and became the second leading news story nationwide; it is estimated 50,000 people found a new experience in Christ as a result of this revival and witness teams that went out from it.

-In **March 1958** a student fast/prayer meeting spilled over into chapel and lasted for 63 hours.

-In **February 1970** student confession and testimonies led to 144 hours of unbroken revival; some 2,000 witness teams went out from Asbury to Churches, cities, and at least 130 college campuses around the nation over the next year.

-In **March 1992** a student confession during the closing chapel of the annual Holiness Conference turned into 127 consecutive hours of prayer and praise.

-In **February 2006** a student chapel led to four days of continuous prayer and praise.

Prayers for The Third (Next) Great Awakening

Here are my prayers for interruption in this generation of young people in America. Will you pray these with me as you read them?

"I do not doubt in the darkness what God gives me in the light"
God needs to interrupt our lives with an undeniable flash of light as He did Paul on the road to Damascus (Acts 9). It doesn't matter how bad it looks. We need to develop a *fighter mentality* in the snowflakes when they face a culture that seems to dim their light. Just because it may not seem like it, God is still moving and the light is always brighter than the darkness.

Keep your faith lit when it is darkest around you by reading, praying, fasting, worship, and speaking the things you want to see.

"God, move. And God, move me!"
The one thing we must understand is that an Awakening or revival is not a method or a combination or a riddle to be solved. There really isn't an equation. I mean, there are things that are precursors to Awakenings and I believe we can move the will of God. But, it still requires a sovereign move of God. God needs to interrupt our lives and bring a sovereign move of His will. When it is needed, He will certainly release a move of the Spirit. Life is His will. And where there is death, His Spirit is ready and willing to send abundant life to replace the darkness upon a land.

> *God is already moving. And I think He really wants us to move also. Maybe our prayer needs to change from "God, move!" And the prayer we should be praying is, "God, move me!"*

"Help us to know the power of repentance and confession"
God needs to interrupt our lives with deep conviction. This may be the most under-appreciated aspect of Christianity. In a world where "I'm OK, You're OK", pop psychology has kept us from admitting our need for a Savior.

So we change our language of "sin" and give it nicknames we can live with that are more comfortable. Like saying that our sin or disobedience to God is nothing but addictions, or struggles, or weaknesses, or issues. Something sterile. When it is actually sin, disobedience, corruption, and unrighteousness. Repentance of sin is the key to Awakenings and revival now. Because it was the key to Awakenings and revival in the past. That hasn't changed.

"For our young people to see the power of God break the oppression of Satan"
God needs to interrupt our lives with His power. Authority is needed in the face of Satanic opposition upon this nation. The Reproductive Health Act, the Re-definition of Marriage, the anger in government, the violence in our nation, and the sexual revolution have each placed their footprint on the sands of time. At some point the Church must drop to her knees and ask for God's power to break the oppression of Satan on this nation.

Throughout scripture Satan has opposed Adam, Eve, Noah, David, John, Peter, Paul, and even Jesus. This Satanic oppression can only be met with the authority of young believers in heavenly opposition.

"God I know you desire faithfulness – but I'm praying it will happen suddenly"
I know there are things that require time and most of Scripture is a constitution for faithfulness. But, there are moments in scripture where everything changed suddenly. I've been asking God would use one miracle. I've been asking God would use one service. I've been asking God would use one person. I've been asking God would use one moment.

This is what is so exciting about God and His interruptions. It could happen at any moment. The exciting part of prayer is we never know when it might happen.

"Send supernatural signs and wonders that are undeniable"
In a generation familiar with the supernatural the church is foreign to it. We must discover the supernatural in our faith again. The very foundation of our faith is based upon the supernatural. See all of the works of Christ in the gospels, see the resurrection of Christ from the dead, and see the unthinkable kingdom of heaven that awaits us. Christianity is supernatural. We need to ask God as a generation for the greatest works of the kingdom to happen in our day.

Could it be the born generational trait of Gen Z may be the key to a generation experiencing Awakening?

"Divine interruptions in our YTH services and in our daily lives"

Don't get confused with the word service. I mean this in two respects. In the gatherings and rallies we have on a weekly basis, and, in our lives outside of the church on a daily basis. I've been asking every YTH group in America would have moments where the Holy Spirit is undeniably in their presence. Both in the weekly gathering and our daily going. Every church and every campus. Every home and every workplace. If America will see another Great Awakening we need an interruption from the Holy Spirit in our daily lives.

Desperate times call for desperate measures. What greater place for this to happen than amongst a generation who is familiar with the supernatural.

Stories of Interruption Again

Look at the stories of young people in your YTH ministry.

I've seen it all over America. There is power in the interruption of suddenlies into our life. And this is why I believe so much in this generation. How quickly God can move. We call it "mojo". Or, when a team "get's on a roll". A basketball team has a 16-2 "run". And the other team calls a timeout. Or when a running back in a football game is running downhill and gaining yards easily. It has happened throughout history. Other terms that describe this include viral, epidemic, pandemic, contagious, rapid, impulsive, and instant.

As we said at the beginning of this chapter, there are Tipping Points in organizations, and in nations, and often in the lives of people. I have seen sudden changes in young people many times. These are students that experienced drastic change, or a revolution, or an overthrow of ideas. A shift or sudden turn. Let these stories encourage you to see the same in the young people around you.

A weekend retreat to Cedar Point, Sandusky Ohio. (This could take a whole chapter)
I was only at the church in Grand Rapids, MI for two months. But that summer we planned a first event to build relationships. As we were headed to a theme park overnighter with about 90 students and leaders, the war started. A war that was about to change everything. When all hell broke loose – well, you might say all of heaven began one of the great setups I've ever seen. So many young people could attest to what was about to happen on this weekend retreat and how it would change their lives.

On a 5 hour trip to the amusement park in Ohio, the bus broke down about 4 hours into the trip and we were in a garage in the middle of nowhere for the better part of the day. By the time we had our transportation solved, the students only had a few hours that evening at the park. And then the tornado hit. Ha Ha. For real.

As this storm came raging into the area, we had to leave the park because it was going to be closed. I had called a church because our hotel was being closed because of the storm also, so we headed back to the church where we had to stay. We would spend the next two days in this church with 90 students and leaders – and one shower.

But the intercession, the worship, the relationship building that took place in those hours of a spontaneous retreat would change everyone's life.

So many ministry leaders around the country today who were not headed to ministry were radically changed on the trip.

An 18 year old young man in Kokomo, IN.
An alternative drug addict/alcoholic teen who was converted in our YTH ministry on a Wednesday night came to meet with me in the office on Thursday morning after the YTH service. As we talked about his conversion and prayed together, we hugged and he left my office. It was about 6 hours later that day I would get a call from his mother that he died in a tragic car accident that afternoon. As his mother spoke with me, she thanked me and shared that he had told her he had gone to Church the night before and given his life to Christ.

A 14 year old in Las Vegas, Nevada.
This young lady came to a YTH Convention and God radically changed her life. Her mom was a prostitute and she didn't want to follow in that lifestyle so when she got home from the convention she told her mom what had happened and was kicked out of the home. She moved in with a YTH Pastor and his family. Just two weeks after the convention I received a letter from the YTH Pastor telling me she had been killed in a car accident. But hadn't missed Church since the convention and was all in with the right friends before her sudden death.

A sophomore boy from Wyoming.

He came to a summer camp as an atheist. He had never been to church for a wedding or a funeral. The YTH ministry that brought him tried to get him to come often but he would never attend their YTH group. Finally, just days before camp they told him they would be playing football at camp. Well, that got him interested. On the first night of camp he was seated in a crowd that did not come forward to the front for worship. About halfway through the worship set he began to become emotional and to talk to several of his friends about what he was experiencing.

He sat through the message that night and at the end of the message he walked forward with the YTH pastor and told me he had given his life to Christ during worship while talking to his friends. He told me he had an argument for everything I was saying because his parents taught him how to defend himself against Christianity. When I asked him why he was so emotional and decided to come forward and give his life to God his answer was simple.

He looked me in the eye and said to me, "I had an argument for all of the things you spoke about. But I did not have an argument for His presence during worship."

This was easily one of the most remarkable revelations about the immediacy of God working in our lives.

I'm sure you have many stories also. I love to retell these because it keeps me fresh and reminds me how God is working in this generation. Maybe you need to take some time and retell to yourself or give some time in the YTH service for all of the stories you have seen in the students around you. I believe God is moving more than we can imagine.

God, do it again and again and again.

Action Steps

- *How can you create "Tipping Points" around your ministry? That might be going to camp, conventions, conferences, mission's trips, or having spiritual emphasis series for renewal and Awakening.*
- *Do a thorough study of the generational traits of the Millennial and the Gen Z sets. Remember the traits we dealt with and use the following practical ideas to appeal to these set traits: Supernatural, Risk-taking, Publishers, Cause-oriented, Teamwork, and the Entrepreneurial vision of the teenagers in this generational set.*
- *How can you and your team sync the YTH ministry setting with each of these traits in your young people?*
- *Review the history of Awakenings with your students so they can see the kind of heritage that the church and YTH ministry have*
- *Review the stories of the students in your YTH ministry and celebrate what God is doing in their lives. Do a video or live student spotlight weekly and watch the culture of the YTH ministry explode with story.*
- *Are you setting aside enough time and space for an interruption in your YTH ministry? Be careful of over-planning and not allowing the Holy Spirit to have room to move in our students lives.*

"Old age realizes the dreams of YTH:
look at the man who built the first insane asylum for the insane;
in his old age he was himself an inmate."

-Soren Kierkegaard

Chapter 6

How YTH Ministry Could Fail the Church

Failure is not always a bad thing. Unless you repeat the same failure over and again.

When I was young I wanted to be an NBA Coach. Probably because I knew I wasn't good enough to play in the league, but, more so because I really thought I had the social skills to handle the players and the acumen to call the game. Maybe you wanted to become a police officer, or a fire fighter, or the President of the United States. When we were young we wanted to change the world. What are we dreaming about today? And how could that dream become a reality for us in real life? If old age really does become our realized dream, how does that fare for us? Or the world?

Maybe reading this book, and this chapter in particular, and seeing this quote will help to make you think about the impact of your dreams and your life. About whether you leave the world a better place or not. Hopefully this chapter will stir in you the desire to dream a dream or create a YTH ministry that is transformative for the church and culture.

YTH ministry is the engine for the sustainability of the church and every organization. The young people we work with will bring the ideas and become the workforce for every institution in their future. That is why I say YTH leaders are the critical piece to the sustainability of the church. If we are not careful, YTH ministry could fail the church by producing unhealthy leadership that produces unhealthy students. And ultimately, an unhealthy future for the church.

Hopefully you want to become a winning YTH leader. With this in mind, let's look at some ways we as YTH leaders could fail the church if we are not careful.

Here are 7 ways YTH ministry could fail the Church:

Unhealthy YTH Leaders

Healthy YTH leaders build healthy YTH ministry. And unhealthy YTH leaders build unhealthy YTH ministry. There is a difference between *'busyness'* and *'business'*. When YTH leaders are busy in the Church, they burn out. Because they spend more time in programming and gaming than they do in relationships and study. When YTH leaders are about the business of the Church, they burn on. Because they spend more time in relationships and study than they do in programming and gaming. It really is simple. Our busyness is not always for the right things. But when it is for the business (or the reason) of the Church, it is for the right things.

> *An unhealthy YTH leader will produce unhealthy students, and ultimately, an unhealthy generation who will lead the church into an unhealthy future.*

Before a YTH leader teaches or preaches to their leaders and students, they must internalize the message they have been preparing. Our personal spiritual health is elementary to us leading others in their corporate spiritual health. One of the missing pieces in leadership development is self-leadership. Because it is easier to lead others than it is to lead ourselves. Create your own personal disciplines before you challenge others to create theirs.

Our own ceilings and lids can become detected by those around us when we have expectations for others we do not have for ourselves. It is easy to expect more from everyone else while we are quite gracious and expect much less of ourselves. Spiritual leadership will deal with the man (woman) before the message.

Self-leadership

Self-leadership is the most difficult kind of leadership. It is much easier to lead others than it is to lead ourselves. But the way in which we lead ourselves has a lot to do with our personal health as a leader.

There are many ways to make this easier. There are ways we can prepare ourselves as YTH leaders to be healthy. It may be a set time of *daily* Bible reading and prayer, *weekly* fasting, *monthly* witnessing or evangelizing or sharing our faith, having *annual* mentors in our life, or committing to a *lifetime* of sexual purity. Did you see that progression? These are disciplines we create from a daily, weekly, monthly, annual, and lifetime commitment. If we expect our followers to live at a certain level of commitment to Christ and the church, then they must see us model in our own lives a certain level of commitment to Christ and the church.

Look at the books on your desk. What I see around the country as I am in leader's offices are a lot of books on leading the team, or leading the organization, or leadership systems and paradigms, or leadership relational competency, social dynamics, and even leadership enneagrams now. But, what I have too often noticed is a lack of personal leadership or spiritual leadership books. I believe what is sitting on your desk or populating your bookshelves are what is most important to you.

Take note of this. If you lack personal spiritual leadership books they need to become your next purchase. You can find a list of those on our website blog.

Healthy YTH leaders will create healthy YTH ministries that create healthy students. This responsibility is our own as leaders. This is not my spouse's faith, my children's faith, my church's faith, or the faith of my denomination. This is my faith and I must possess it with spiritual health.

Healthy relationships

Unhealthy relationships is one of the outcomes of unhealthy leaders. This can be clearly seen in our abuse of our authority or title over younger people. There is a great responsibility to not take advantage of the teenagers we work with.

Let me address the practical part of leading young people – specifically of the opposite sex. I know there are as many concerns today leading people of the same sex also. I will deal with this here also. Either way, as leaders we could be tempted to lead young people in a domineering way. That kind of controlling authority that comes with a leadership title is a dangerous thing in the hands of unhealthy leaders. So here are a few practical tips to help you with this:

> *I have been in YTH ministry for 36 years now and not once has a student brought an accusation against me. Not once have I crossed the line of disrespect or lust or power. Not because I am perfect. But because of two things: my personal spiritual principles and practices, and, the grace of God.*

I am sure the students and leaders who came up under our YTH ministry would overwhelmingly say we set an atmosphere of love and acceptance – without crossing the line. Yes, I would squeeze the students. I would look them in the eye and tell them I loved them. But I always had parameters and guidelines for this.

We must have practices that protect our principles of relationship. Here are a few of those practices:

- I never gave a teenage girl or female leader a ride in my car. For any reason. In fact, to this day, the only three girls in the world who have been in a car alone with me since I have been in ministry is my mom, my wife, and my daughter.
- Another practice that protected my principles was keeping my door open when a student was in my office
- It is very important to instruct your admin or spouse to call in or knock on the door of your office during an appointment
- We should never show affection in private
- I would never show affection to a teenager Jane would identify to me because she felt discernment toward a certain person
- After appointments I will always speak with someone about the appointment
- For many years I kept a journal of every appointment. The notes after the appointment could then be read by anyone I would need to share them with.

These are just a few of the many safeties that can guard your integrity. Remember, most of us do not wake up in the morning and expect to fail. But if we have practices that protect our principles it will help to fight against the schemes of Satan, and, the temptations that can come as a result of our lack of discipline in our own life.

A Loss of Contextual YTH Ministry

Another way YTH ministry can fail the church is to lose our context. I want to look at two concepts here. The concepts of missiology and ecology.

Missiology is the study of mission and the forms, methods, or the purpose of why we do something. Understanding the why of anything is key to its success. Every organization is driven by the why. And every successful leader can tell you their why. This definitely relates to the philosophy of ministry we will talk about in this chapter also, but, it is deeper than just an approach. Foremost in the success of YTH ministry philosophy must be the why. I see the why for YTH ministry as bringing the gospel to the context. The setting.

> *Effective YTH ministry is sharing the gospel to teenagers within the context of the YTH setting. Effective YTH ministry cannot merely be done then within the walls of the church.*

Ecology is the study of individuals and things within their context or surroundings and how they relate to each other in a certain culture. An ecology is measured by how a population or community relates to and interacts in the same environment. Ecology and missiology are best studied together. When these are studied side-by-side, we gain great understanding of social settings in society.

YTH leaders should be the greatest sociologists on the planet. Because they understand the times and they know what to do. That is the tribal trait of the sons of Issachar, one of the tribes of Israel. You can read about Issachar's place in Israel in 1 Chronicles 12.

Neutral site ministry

While speaking with Dick Brogden one morning on a short flight from Springfield, MO to Chicago, IL, we were talking about YTH ministry. Dick and his wife Jenn and two boys, Luke and Zack, founded the global LiveDead missionary movement. Jenn was also in my YTH group and was my admin for a couple of years. So we have been close for many years. On this short flight we were talking about how each other was doing and catching up.

As we got into YTH ministry, Dick said something that was matter of fact, but, registered with me right away. I think I checked out of the conversation for a few minutes as I thought about YTH ministry across the country and their commitment to campus. He said, "If a missionary came and looked at how U.S. YTH ministry happens, they would scratch their head and ask, '*Why are you not on campus?*'"

I loved it. Of course, I wanted to hug him for saying it. Why? Because to a missionary it makes sense the campus is the place where the target is shaped the most. I think it goes without saying that the campus represents the teen setting or the teen culture – and yet the teen setting is not just the middle school or the high school building. In order for us to do effective YTH ministry, we must have a presence in the whole teen setting.

The whole YTH ministry setting is the teen context outside of the church building. A complete missiology of YTH ministry intends its programming in the church and the cultural settings. A proper ecology of the YTH culture places every YTH ministry in the context of teenagers.

> *The future of effective YTH ministry will be determined by our neutral site presence. This would include the school campus, extracurricular activities, and the social hangouts of teenagers such as sporting events, the mall, and the work place. This will look like YTH leaders being seen in the setting of students on a regular basis. I used to announce to our students which events or games I would be at each week. This builds the contextual relationship between the church and the teenager.*

We cannot do YTH ministry solely on the church grounds. That will only help to create codependent students. Remember, by far, most of the miracles in the New Testament happened outside of the temple and in the marketplace, the homes, and the countryside. Effective YTH ministry should be doing ministry in the same way as the 1st century in many ways – outside of the temple setting.

Mono-Strategy for Reaching a Diverse Student

There are many models (or strategies, approaches, or philosophies) to YTH ministry. The YTH Service, Discipleship, Outreach, Small Group, Fine Arts, Events, and even Campus-based models are all popular. To simply emphasize one of these approaches is limiting. The diversity in the YTH culture demands we become proficient in multiple models. Or it will be difficult to speak into the context of a specific sociological set like the millennial and Gen Z. It takes all kinds and types of people to reach all kinds and types of people.

For instance, if your entire YTH ministry model is Evangelism and Outreach with a Campus-based philosophy, then you must couple that methodology with Discipleship. Or you will have a very shallow and immature YTH ministry. In the same way, if you have a Discipleship and Small Group-based philosophy, then you must couple that with an Evangelism and Outreach model also. Or you will have an internalized ministry. The best practice for YTH ministry development is a multi-strategy approach. Multi-strategy YTH ministry is healthy because it focuses on a more holistic approach to ministry.

> Look at the YTH tribes present in our society: athletes, brainiacs, alternatives, home-school, politicals, globals, artisans, and preps. We must have a variety of leaders and methods and approaches in our YTH ministry if we are going to reach a variety of people. It takes all kinds and types of people to reach all kinds and types of people.

If we are honest, most YTH ministries are able (or willing) to function in 1 or 2 of these approaches. Maybe a good YTH Service and a Worship and Presence-based model. Or, capable Small Groups and Student Leadership development. However, because these two examples are so similar in their approach, there will need to be an additional emphasis on an incongruent approach such as periodic visits to the Campus and/or Fine Arts coupled with this. In other words, a healthy YTH ministry will exhibit a variety of strategies that create a diverse and healthy environment.

In a mono-strategy YTH ministry there is little adaptation and breadth to the culture and it can become narrow in its focus and its outcomes. What a multi-strategy approach does is widen the possibility of reaching more students within a sector, and, engage the gifts and talents of more people assuring shared ownership.

Each YTH leader or ministry will have a core competency commitment in one or even two of these strategies. But, the YTH leader or YTH ministry who can become proficient in 3 or 4 of these models can have a greater opportunity to reach and disciple more students. And that requires YTH leaders to have varied skills and multiple gifted leaders around them. For instance, if every one of my YTH leaders are jocks we are going to reach a lot of athletes. But, the artisans may not feel as welcome if every message, event, or conversation is about sports and athletics. You can relate this multi-strategy analogy to every sector of teenage culture.

A healthy YTH ministry values a multi-strategy approach to leadership because it values reaching all kinds of students.

A Loss of the Veteran and Rookie Relationship in YTH Ministry

The mentoring relationship between the young YTH leader and the experienced YTH leader is vital to a healthy YTH ministry and church. In my travels and conversations with so many leaders across the country I have seen an unfortunate relationship between the two emerge. The young leader can often think the vets are stuck in the scriptures and don't understand culture – they are dinosaurs who preach a gospel society isn't interested in and they are living on past successes from 2 or 3 decades ago. On the other hand, the veteran leader can think the rookie is into cultural trends and doesn't understand scripture – they are hipsters who preach gaming and videos with more gaga ball and charades than they do biblical content.

Both of these views are unbalanced and extreme.

What we need are young YTH leaders who *honor* the wisdom of the veteran YTH leaders, and, veteran YTH leaders who *value* the resources of the young YTH leaders. As a veteran of 36 years of YTH ministry, I will be the first to say I have not attained YTH ministry perfection. I still love to have conversations with the rookies and see the passion in their eyes and the new ideas they have.

But, if the young leaders will listen, the veteran YTH leaders have so many lessons learned through decades of experience they can impart to the rookies. If they will listen, it could help them to do so much more than my generation of YTH leaders ever did.

> *My ceiling is their floor. I am not interested in just sitting around and telling stories about the past – to walk young leaders through my museum of memories. NO! I want to walk alongside of younger YTH leaders and build new memories together. I am so much more interested in movements than museums. If the younger YTH leaders in America do not do greater things than my generation, we have failed them.*

Practical Relationship Between Veterans and Rookies

Here are a few ways we can promote the veteran and rookie relationship in YTH ministry:

1. Mentoring Relationships
We can see this happening around the country in *programs* like *The Cadre* in Atlanta, GA. The Cadre YTH leadership training of Jeanne Mayo has trained over one thousand YTH leaders across the country. What is so significant about this is that Jeanne Mayo has been in YTH ministry for five decades. Acclaimed by Ministries Today as "America's Number One Youth Pastor," Jeanne has thrown her heart and passion into YTH ministry as reflected in her life mission statement: "The motivation and mentorship of Kamikaze Christianity into practicing and potential Kingdom champions." She has taken 5 different YTH ministries from handfuls to hundreds; and even today, she is still actively in the trenches and on staff at Victory Church, a thriving church of over 16,000. (1)

In recent years, Jeanne founded Youth Leader's Coach, a non-profit organization that seeks "to instruct, equip, inspire and encourage the youth pastors and youth leaders of this generation." Through this venue, The Cadre was formed and a new generation of YTH leaders have been able to learn from one of the best. When I see reports of these Cadre meetings it is so encouraging to see young leaders listening to Jeanne's veteran voice. It is this kind of veteran and rookie relationship so vital to the handoff of YTH ministry from one generation to the next.

2. Denominational Relationships
This veteran and rookie relationship can also be easily facilitated by *denominational programs and leadership resourcing*. That might be events, training, resources, or organic relationship. This strategic denominational relationship can create inter-generational leadership mentoring between the local church setting and the more experienced denominational YTH leadership. The denominational relationship can mature younger YTH leaders – especially in the local setting with volunteer YTH leaders who may not have the training or the resources.

3. Local Relationships
There are also *local level relationships* where you can find veteran YTH leadership at other churches or organizations. This could be convenient because they are close and have similar

setting or environment traits that can make the relationship natural. One of the things I did as a YTH pastor was to build local relationships inter-denominationally with YTH leaders in my city. Watching these veterans when I was young gave me ideas and goals to work for. This could include local church YTH leaders, para-church organizations, and even school faculty and staff.

4. Public School Relationships
The *public school* has many veterans in YTH work. Over the years I have learned some of my best leaders were in the public school system – I have had quality teachers, coaches, counselors, principals, and superintendent relationships that I have learned from. For the most part, school leadership is in this for the right reasons. Another advantage with public school relationships is the access it gives you to the school campus. That can be a game changer. These are great people with many resources to learn from in your area.

5. Regional or National Leadership Conference Relationships
If you want to take the ceiling off and extend the fences of your ministry there is nothing like a *Regional or National YTH leadership Convention.* These kind of movements are a great way to increase learning quickly. A growing popular environment, the larger regional or national conferences that specialize on YTH ministry have a lot of veterans who are used to this setting and understand the role they have in the handoff of YTH ministry to the next generation of leaders. One of the things I enjoy about these settings is the interdenominational makeup of these venues that allows training in varying strategic and theological and diverse settings.

The rookie and the veteran YTH leader relationships must be a priority for the church. A healthy future of YTH ministry is dependent upon this generational handoff.

Poor YTH Ministry Ecclesiology

Ecclesiology is basically the study of the Church. I like to call it *applied theology in the human setting.* YTH ministry must do great ecclesiology if it is going to be successful in the 21st century. A focus upon slick Wednesday night (or whatever night you meet) programming and pulling off one exciting event each quarter will produce shallow students who will shed the church as soon as they graduate from High School because they missed one of the most important faith developers – theology in community. And when this happens, the faith never becomes theirs.

Many YTH leaders fail to think through the big picture of theology and faith. Because they spend more time on culture and hype. It is the responsibility of the YTH team to be strategic in the connecting and retention of students into the church body. YTH leaders who simply build a sub-culture of YTH ministry separate from the whole church are missing the rewards that could arise from inter-generational relationship and connection.

The Christian faith is best passed along from one generation to the next in a community-based relationship. Psalm 78 is our great example of ecclesiology – the faith story is shared from one era to the next. This takes proximity.

I love what Pamela Erwin, longtime YTH minister and educator, said on this topic of ecclesiology and context.

> *"Religious environments can foster positive spiritual development in adolescents. Spirituality relates to the developmental processes in which a young person searches for meaning and purpose and wrestles with questions that transcend their mindset."* (2)

This process of discipleship and spiritual progeny explodes in good ecclesiology. Where there is an environment in YTH ministry of intentional culture-building and practical theology among peers, faith formation happens.

Intergenerational Ecclesiology

Inter-generational proximity is rewarding. It assures the faith handoff, increases unity in the church, is the direct cause of sustainability for the church, develops spiritual formation and maturity in the younger generation, and gives a re-purpose to the adults in the church. Isolation and creating a sub-group is never the answer for YTH ministry.

If we are going to increase maturity and retention of our young people, it will take intentional ecclesiology to build these next leaders of the church. It should be clearly understood by the entire church that the future pastors, elders, deacons, department leaders, and administrative staff are coming from within the Next Gen ministry. It is detrimental to do YTH ministry in isolation of the Church.

- This might look like having every level of leader in the church, no matter the department, in relationship with a different department
- Or it may look like the older leaders in the church having a protégé or mentor relationship with young people
- This may be as simple as a series of teachings on inter-generational worship and discipleship every year and creating this culture in the whole church
- An inter-generational setting could also be accomplished by the YTH pastor periodically inviting the lead pastor of the church into the YTH ministry setting
- This may also be done by not removing teenagers from the all-church setting on the weekends and encouraging them to become a part of the volunteer pool of the church

The church should be able to connect the adults and teenagers in the same setting or our ecclesiology is useless. This disconnect is dangerous to the future of the church. YTH ministry that has a plan for ecclesiology will assure the sustainability of the church for generations to come.

A Lack of Supernatural Leadership

Christianity is nothing if it is not supernatural. From Genesis 1 to Revelation 22 there is a supernatural narrative in scripture that lays the foundation for our faith. Couple this biblical narrative with the love for the supernatural in Gen Z and we have an explosive relationship.

All of the sociological studies call this generation out on their love for the supernatural.

In James Emory White's *The Rise of the Nones*, the "nones" are described as the "religiously unaffiliated". When asked about their religion on various surveys or polls, they responded "I'm nothing". And their numbers are rising faster than any other group. As a matter fact, the highest percentage of atheists is found in the Gen Z set. This is certainly a result of Christianity losing its supernatural message. But, even with all of the research, it is clear they are still drawn to the supernatural – a journey that could certainly lead them to Christianity. (3)

Need some proof of this? Look at the social following of the supernatural. Now a whole new generation of teens are intrigued by the other world. Recent findings from Pinterest say pins relating to witchcraft are up by +281% among Gen Z; that's over three times more than millennials. The hashtag #witchesofinstagram has over 1.9 milllion posts and there are a plethora of Gen Z 'witchfluencers' like 21-year-old Harmony Nice from Norwich; who has a YouTube following of nearly half-a-million, as well as a book deal. (4)

> *These reports serve to prove YTH ministry must become comfortable with the supernatural. The world is familiar with the supernatural but the church is foreign to it. How did we get here? Christianity is nothing if it is not supernatural.*

Look at the scriptures.

In the Old Testament Moses' leadership was marked by the supernatural. Esther too. The works of Elijah and Elisha are undeniable. It was said of King David that he governed Israel with the integrity of his heart and the skillfulness of his hands and he surpassed King Saul in exploits. If you were to detail the ways God used David and his mighty men it would be a major bestseller. King Josiah was 8 years old when he became king, and by the time he was 16 he had removed all of the national idols. Who could forget the mighty exploits of Samson and Daniel and the prophets?

In the New Testament, the disciples were used to do some pretty amazing things. Stories of each of them and their demonstrations in the Spirit fill the gospels with so many signs and wonders. Paul the Apostle placed a great emphasis upon natural and spiritual leadership by stating they could not be separated. Paul saw many signs and wonders among the Jews and the Gentiles.

Even Jesus said we would do greater things than He did if we would only believe. All of these examples are evidence of the importance of supernatural leadership and this plays right into the characteristic trait of this generation. What an explosive relationship between a sociological trait and a theological truth.

The Holy Spirit and Spiritual Leadership

There is no doubt YTH leaders must have natural communication, administrative, and relational skill-sets. Storytelling is important to reach this YTH culture. Creativity is elementary to this generation. Personality is magnetic. But, these are not sufficient enough to build a remarkable and lasting ministry. Especially in the wake of a dynamic movie and special effects industry. There must be a greater emphasis from YTH leaders to walk in Spiritual Leadership by seeking the gifts of the Holy Spirit to help build the Church. Do you think the Holy Spirit is intimidated by Hollywood?

> *There are no less than 33 supernatural themed movies and television shows out right now. And this testifies to the interest of our generation. If there is one enviable trait the Millennial and Gen Z sets would desire in the Church, it is the supernatural.*

Since we cannot deny the central theme of the supernatural in American culture, then we must believe God for the same in the church. You cannot get away from the supernatural theme in our society and same should be said of the church also. This is part of the generational traits of Millennial and Gen Z sets and it should be part of the theological traits of the church.

While the world is familiar with the supernatural, the church has been foreign to it. If this changes in the church today, we may have one of the best apologetic tools to reach this generation because the supernatural is in the DNA of the church and its message.

Here are a few questions surrounding this area:

- *Do you have a spiritually disciplined life as a YTH leader?*
- *Are we teaching our students how to pray and fast?*
- *Do you have a prayer meeting for the YTH ministry?*
- *Have you created a series on the miracles in the bible?*
- *Do you allow for a time of prayer and waiting in the YTH setting to believe God for signs and wonders?*
- *Have you ever instructed students in how to operate in the supernatural gifts of the Spirit?*

- *Are you willing to set time aside to do this and take students to the streets to pray with people?*

We have under-challenged God and teenagers in this area. I've learned miracles start taking place when we ask for them. Maybe we're not seeing the supernatural in our YTH ministry because we are not living, as Jesus said to the disciples, a supernatural "this kind" of life as a leader. If the future of the church is in the hands of the young people in our YTH ministry, we should be placing much more thought and strategic planning on the supernatural in the church.

The church cannot apologize for the supernatural. The supernatural may be one of the greatest tools we have to reach this present generation.

Loss of Proximal Human Relations

In order for all of this to take place, YTH ministry will need to model relationship and a neighborhood mentality. It is not enough for YTH leaders to lead from the platform or the office. We must be leaders who are present in the teen context because even though teenagers are the most glocally connected generation, they still lack human relations. A priority for the future of YTH ministry must be the proximity of leaders and students in authentic relationships in and out of the church setting.

There are so many ways to practice this proximal connection in the YTH ministry.

-I would suggest learning the names and stories of students if the church is going to become relative to teenagers.
-One of the great ways to promote human relations and adult and student connection is to have a spotlight every week introducing a student to the group. Take the time to interview students and share their story each week.
-Another way we can connect with students is through our social media as YTH leaders. Our social media and technology ethic could fail to counter the onslaught of losing teenagers to the screen and a faux world online.
-We must build *interrelated communities* where human relations is central to the culture and not *isolated communities* where human relations is secondary.

Christian YTH ministry is nothing if it is not human relations.

Maybe the most prophetic statement about the technological age was given by Martin Luther King, Jr. in 1965. He was speaking to the imbalance of technology and theology that we would see. David Kinnaman, of the Barna Group, describes the prophetic word from King, Jr. to America:

> "Yes, there's the rub: instant access to information is not wisdom. In a 1965 sermon, Dr. Martin Luther King Jr. could have been talking about our present moment when he asked, "How much of our modern life can be summarized in that arresting dictum of the poet Thoreau, 'Improved means to an unimproved end'? . . . We have allowed our technology to outdistance our theology and for this reason we find ourselves caught up with many problems." (5)

Pop-Ups (Live Social Events) and YTH Ministry in the Wild

Look at the technology advances happening now. AI & Hologram phones are a reality if they can fix battery life. Can you imagine the problem of phone use when AI and Hologram phones become standard? What about issues such as sexting or driving when hologram phones hit the market? Fighting the rise of technology is like the proverbial ant in front of the train. We cannot stop the growth of social media and other forms of technology such as AI and hologram phones, but, we can start a disciplined use of it.

So maybe fighting it is not the answer. How about redeeming social media and technology? Proximal relationship can solve the overuse of teen social media and become a replacement for distal relationships caused by students pulling away from interaction.

The fact is, social media is not going away. Every YTH ministry must make it a priority to have a human relations plan for their students in the wake of social media. Including things like promotional and YTH group materials available to the students for posting and story on social media. This could look like creating images for students to use in their social platforms to increase the footprint of the YTH series or even for the promotion of a YTH event. With the digital information available, YTH ministry could easily become viral with a few strategic plans.

Aside from just the sermon or series images, the social image identity is important also. That would include doing more live social media events and pop-ups to help create YTH ministry in the wild! Another important aspect of the social image is YTH merch such as clothing, hats, stickers, and other items that create identity, culture, and footprint. This kind of live or graphic human relations is a critical part of helping students go public with their faith.

The needed relational capital must become a central elementary priority in YTH ministry. Proximity must become something we are known for. We cannot trade program for proximity.

Finally

If we are not careful to deal with these 7 failures, we will continue to place unhealthy YTH leadership in roles that influence a generation of unhealthy students who will then lead an unhealthy church in years to come. The future sustainability of the church is dependent upon healthy YTH leadership. Make it a priority to not repeat the failures of the past. But to learn from them and to assure a successful church because of a healthy YTH ministry.

Action Steps

Healthy YTH ministry will take a major commitment. Use these talking points to assess the health of your YTH ministry and how it is affecting the church and the community around you.

- *Are you modeling only one form or philosophy of YTH ministry or have you intentionally broadened your forms of reaching and discipling students? For example, mix between discipleship & outreach and programming & presence based structures.*
- *To appeal and attract a diverse adolescent, you need a diverse leadership team*
- *Have you considered YTH ministry as a life calling?*
- *Have you had a veteran YTH leader sit with your team before? This should be done every year.*
- *Create a series of teachings on inter-generational worship and discipleship every year*
- *How many times has your Lead Pastor been in the YTH setting? Inviting the lead into the YTH ministry setting brings continuity.*
- *Do your students serve on weekends in the church services? Don't remove teens from adult church setting.*
- *Have we modeled spiritual discipline in our life as a YTH leader?*
- *Do you have a prayer meeting for the YTH ministry?*
- *Have you created a series of the miracles in the bible? Do you allow for a time of prayer in the YTH setting to believe God for signs and wonders?*
- *How often are you involved in student's lives as a YTH leader?*
- *Create promotional YTH group materials available to the students for posting on social media. This could look like creating images for students to use in their social platforms to increase the footprint of the YTH series or the promotion of a YTH event.*
- *Doing live social media events and pop-ups to help create YTH ministry in the wild*
- *Another important aspect of the social image is YTH merch. Clothing, hats, stickers, and other items can create identity, culture, and footprint.*

"We need to do whatever it takes
to get our children together and pay attention to them.
Because that's our future.
What's in the hearts and minds of our children
is what's in our future."
-Louis Gossett, Jr.

Chapter 7

The Future of YTH Ministry

The impact of 2.5 million Christian teenagers on America could be the most significant happening in our nation's history – or it could be the most insignificant happening in our nation's history

"We live in a decaying age. Young people no longer respect their parents. They are rude and impatient. They frequently inhabit taverns and Inns and have no self-control."
(Inscribed on a 5,000-year-old Egyptian tomb)

"What is happening to our young people? The offspring will not be well-born or fortunate. To be sure, being unworthy, as guardians begin to neglect them, paying too little heed to their music. The youth have in low esteem their teachers as well as their overseers; and, overall, the young copy the elders and contend hotly with them in words and in deeds, disrespect their elders, they disobey their parents. They ignore the law. They riot in the streets, inflamed with wild notions. Their morals are decaying. What is to become of the youth?"
(Plato remarks from The Republic, Book 8, 4th century BC)

"The young people of today think of nothing but themselves. They have no reverence for parents or old age. They are impatient of all restraint...As for the girls, they are forward, immodest and unladylike in speech, behavior and dress."
(Peter the Hermit, 1274)

"Youth were never more saucie, yea never more savagely saucie – the ancient are scorned, the honourable are contemned, the magistrate is not dreaded. Children as they play about the streets have been heard to curse and swear and call one another nick-names."
(The Wise-Man's Forecast, Thomas Barnes 1624)

"What a weary time those young years were – to have this great desire and the need to live, but, not the ability to do so."
(Charles Bukowski, 1920)

A conversation between a little boy and an old man. Said the little boy, "Sometimes I drop my spoon." Said the old man, "I do that too." The little boy whispered, "I wet my pants." The old man whispered, "I do that too," and laughed silently. Said the little boy, "But I often cry." The old man nodded, "So do I young man." "But worst of all," said the boy, "It seems grown-ups don't pay attention to me." And the little boy felt the warmth of a wrinkled old hand upon his head. "I know what you mean," said the old man.
(Shel Silverstein, 1960)

"Youth have trouble making decisions. They would rather hike in the Himalayas than climb a corporate ladder. They have few heroes, no anthems, no style to call their own. They crave entertainment, but their attention span is as short as one zap of a TV dial. And they will be different tomorrow."
(Proceeding with Caution, Time 2001)

"This idea of purity and you're never compromised and you're always politically woke and all that stuff, youth should get over that quickly. The way to bring about change is not to be as judgmental as possible about other people. Then I can sit and feel pretty good about myself because, man, you see how woke I was. That's not activism. If all you're doing is casting stones, you're probably not going to get that far. The world is messy. People who do really good stuff have flaws."
(President Barack Obama to young people on social reform, 2019)

Historically, the history of YTH has been debated – on both the negative and the positive side of the argument. You will always find the crowd who is cheering for them, and, the crowd who is booing them. To be honest, every generation has downed YTH. There's a name for it. It's called *ephebiphobia*, or, "the fear of youth". The negative reports of YTH is widely reported over the years.

Every generation has claimed it was the worst. And yet, if you read the news headlines from 40 years ago, they do not read much different than today. But, as you can sense in these pages - hope, optimism, support, and promise for the Millennial and Gen Z YTH sets abound here.

The Data

With that optimism must rise a plan also. Because when it comes to the numbers of students attending our YTH ministries, we are basically sitting in the same place today as we were 40 years ago. Even with the increase in the number of churches through the church growth movement, we haven't necessarily seen a demonstrated increase in the numbers of YTH coming to the church.

The numbers of teenagers who were attending church in one denomination (the Assemblies of God) in the 1970's was around 330,000. The same denomination is seeing about 380,000 teenagers in attendance today. More on that later. So, aside from several other things, what that actually means is our YTH ministry models may not be working very well.

What does the future of YTH ministry look like? Here are some important questions as we move forward with these numbers in mind and how YTH ministry could affect the future of the church and culture:

-Is YTH ministry as we see it today relevant for the future of the church?
-Why are the theology statistics plummeting in the Millennial and now in the Gen Z sets? Could this be a family problem and not a YTH ministry problem?
-Is there evidence or proof that a specific approach or model of YTH ministry is most effective?
-Is there a YTH ministry approach or model that is to blame for the plummeting statistics?
-Is YTH ministry only growing in the large church?
-Could social media be the trigger for a YTH revival in the church?
-Does YTH ministry have a cultural problem?
-Has YTH ministry slid too far down the cultural hill?
-Does YTH ministry have a message problem?
-What are the most important characteristic traits of Gen Z – atheism, humanitarian, publishers, competitive, diversity – and how should these affect YTH ministry in the future?

We've gone through a lot of different eras and approaches in YTH ministry the last 30 years or so. YTH ministry has gone through many phases in its young history. But the last three phases or emphases would have to include the Presence-based approach, the Program-based approach, and the Social-based approach. Here's a quick definition of the YTH ministry approaches over the past fifty years:

1. An approach on *presence-based* YTH ministry that was more classic and traditional in thought (from the Billy Graham and the Jesus Movement)

2. An approach on *program-based* YTH ministry, campus access, and seeker/postmodern thought (from the Interdenominational and Mega-church movement)

3. An approach on *social-based* YTH ministry and emergent rejection of classic/seeker thought (from the Millennial and now the Gen Z YTH movement)

What is so interesting about these stages or phases over recent YTH ministry history, is that through these years there have been no significant increase in YTH attendance in the church, nor has there been significant YTH group influence and effective outreach to their culture. We will look at the research in just a moment. And while there are some encouraging trends, the data isn't exactly optimistic.

In order to get a clear picture of U.S. teenagers, let's look at four important research data from four different organizations – the U.S. Government, Barna, Pew, and the University of Michigan. Pew Research compiled the following four datasets concerning the following teenage issues. (1)

Center for Disease Control, U.S. Government
- Youths age 12-17 showed a rise of major depression in the past decade from 5% to 12%
- Teenage pregnancy has continued a sharp decline from 61 births in 1,000 girls (1991) to 20 births in 1,000 girls (2016)
- In 2017, 17% of teens were living below the poverty level – down from 19% in 2014
- In the last decade, reported gangs at high schools dropped from 20% to 10%
- The number one cause of death amongst teenagers is unintended deaths (accidents), followed by suicide, and then homicide

Barna Research
- Only 4% of Gen Z have a biblical world view

- Atheism has doubled among teens as compared to the general population
- Only 59% of Gen Z say they are some kind of Christian
- More than 80% believe faith is relevant in their life
- And yet 37% believe it is impossible to know for sure if God is real

Pew Research
- More than 70% of teens say that anxiety is a major problem
- The number one pressure teens face is still education and grades (61%). And only 30% of teens said that "looking good" was a major pressure.
- A large number (81%) of teenagers say helping someone in need is very important to them
- 65% of teenagers think they spend the right amount of time with their parents – 25% say they do not spend enough time with their parents
- And 59% of teenagers say they get a hug from their parents daily

University of Michigan
- Between on campus and cyber bullying, 33% of teens have been bullied in the past 12 months
- The consumption of alcohol among 12th graders is down the past decade from 54% to only 30%
- Marijuana use is up from 13% to 22% among 12th graders
- Vaping has almost doubled among teenagers from 4% to 7% who reported monthly vaping

What is clear from this look at these datasets is that the institution of family has a problem. But, there is another problem we will focus upon. The overall failure of YTH ministry. Our various approaches at YTH ministry have not worked for quite some time.

The Millennial and Gen Z sets are showing the worst spiritual statistical analysis we have seen. And yet, there are many other optimistic trends in the research. What this suggests to me is that even in the worst of times as a society, we have the opportunity before us to shape the present generation of Millennial's and Gen Z to lead America to its greatest days. What we need to do is to take this real data and all of the other things we have talked about in this book and forge a plan.

The first plan is to look at our resource. Our teenagers.

A Sleeping Giant

Given this reality, we need a plan moving forward. You have seen many practical principles at the end of each chapter in this book. There is so much for you to consider and to put into practice. As we close the book out, this chapter will raise the key future ethics that must become common practices in YTH ministry. Hope is on our side. I have seen the optimism in full scope in every setting of our nation – the urban, the suburban, and the rural. I have seen the optimism in full scope in every setting in the church – the small, the medium, and the large church.

The sleeping giant in front of us must be awakened.

If the statistics hold true from the latest Barna research from the Impact 360 study; that 1 in 10 teenagers in America is an engaged Christian – meaning their beliefs and practices are shaped by their faith – then that would be about 1% of about 26 million Junior High and Senior High YTH in our nation. Or about 2.5 million teens who call themselves engaged Christians.

Idealistically speaking, this is an opportunistic number. Sure, it is a low percentage of teenagers in relation to the whole. But, that is 2.5 million teenagers who could help shape *The Third (Next) Great Awakening* in America. How are you going to look at this number?

> *What if YTH ministry could win a generation in America to Christianity and the church instead of losing them to humanism and atheism? What could be the result of a generation of 2.5 million teenagers who are sold out to the cause of Christianity and the Kingdom of God? Do you see the impact of 2.5 million teenagers who are supremely committed to loving Christ and loving mankind?*

The condition of our world speaks for this incredible spiritual loss of the other 24 million lost teenagers, but, I also believe the condition of a whole generational society could be revolutionized rapidly by 2.5 million supremely committed Christian teenagers. Within a single generation! I love how the Impact 360 Report described the future of YTH ministry in the latest Barna research from 2018:

"Teens today, like teens of long ago, wrestle with insecurity, bullying, boredom, loneliness, raging hormones, and paralyzing doubt. They navigate their first crushes, question their parents' beliefs and dream of their own future. Perhaps what adults need first and foremost to remind ourselves is this: we were there once too. They are not so very different from us at that age." (2)

This is a spectacular reminder to all YTH leaders in our work to awaken the sleeping giant. To take the circa 2.5 million Christian teenagers entrusted to us and shape them for the greatest revival in American history. I choose to see this number as a strength and not a weakness. Does that make our work of evangelism easier? Maybe a little at the inspirational level.

What remains is there are a lot of teenagers to reach in our nation and it will only be possible if we loose the 1 out of 10 who are already engaged with Christianity upon their own peers with a tidal wave of supernatural faith. That will take as much dedicated spiritual intention from YTH ministry in the coming 25 years as we modeled the lack of it in the past 25 years.

We can do this. If the Lord tarries.

What crosses everyone's mind in this topic is what YTH ministry will look like in the next 50 years. Will it be much the same? Will it be completely different? Does YTH ministry even exist in 50 years? Could YTH ministry become more inter-denominational locally? What would happen if YTH ministry was turned over to the local para-church organizations? Would anyone try to juvenile the church and become completely Next Gen/YTH-oriented in its approach while offering adult programs in a mid-week setting?

A Futurist View

The reason we have looked at the past in this writing is because of the influence of the past upon the future. What everyone knows is the hardest part about predicting the future is the unpredictable human element. So, we have to understand our past and our present before we can say with any confidence what our future could look like. It is not *easy* to predict the future. But the more data and information we have it is certainly *easier*. Looking at the whole view of YTH ministry history can help us to gain a futurist view.

> *As we said in earlier chapters, the history of YTH ministry is embedded in revival and Awakenings. So, wouldn't it make sense that the future of YTH ministry is embedded in the same kind of movement?*

Let's do a concise review of the history of YTH ministry in America from Chapter 1 and 2. I believe it is much easier to understand the future of something by understanding its past. After looking at these quickly, I will then give you a few of my thoughts on the indeterminate future of our work as YTH leaders.

The 2nd Great Awakening (1790's-1860's) – The mass of YTH who were born again in the 2nd Great Awakening would flood into the church and would require a change in the focus of the church and its ministry to young people

The Sunday School Movement (1790's-1820's) – This weekend emphasis on bible training and reaching out to the children and YTH in the streets would become the initial form of how the church would disciple this new set pouring into the church after the Awakenings

Early para-Church Movement (1820's-1950's) – The church would be forced into the community by Christian organizations who were reaching out to the less fortunate and to the public schools and would ultimately lead the church to an external neutral site emphasis to neighborhoods and organizations

Student Volunteer Movement / College campuses (1860's-1900) – Coming out of the Awakenings, many of the teenagers would end up in university and they would offer their futures to God and the kingdom for a global missionary movement unlike what we have ever seen

Billy Graham Crusades (1930's-1980's) – Young people were looking for a spiritually powerful iconic figure in the church and Graham would be used as an influential voice for many decades in public crusade evangelism that would gain the trust of an entire nation

Jesus Movement (1960's-1970's) - This suddenly would begin on the beaches and in the bars of central California and come at some of the worst days in American history to surprise our nation and its young people with America's most important spiritual moment

Interdenominational Movement/Mega-Church Movement (1980's-2000's) - What this mega-church movement taught us was that social forms and culture could be impacted by the church and its organizational programming and influence

Millennial YTH Movement (2000-2020) - This movement of young people in the church would take the form of cultural influences through social media and other causes to another level, and yet, the spiritual identity of an entire generation would be lost in the milieu

If we defined the history of YTH ministry in a simple way – using the past and the future – we could see it in two streams. The *classic* YTH ministry in the first 150 years, and, the *millennial* YTH ministry in the last 50 years. What can we learn from this 200 year window? And how does this impact the next 50 years of YTH ministry?

Classic YTH Ministry - prayer, worship, preaching, and evangelism

In the first 150 years or so of YTH ministry there would be a raw emphasis of prayer, worship, preaching, and evangelism from the Awakening and the revival atmosphere growing out of the religious movements here in America. Except for a few settings, this classic form of YTH ministry is almost nonexistent today. That is certainly disappointing.

When you look at all of the other YTH ministry approaches over the past 50 years, combined with the plummeting religious data in the last two generational sets, it almost seems obvious a return to these four commitments is part of the answer to the future of YTH ministry.

> *Knowing what I knew then about YTH ministry, and knowing what I know now about YTH ministry, I wouldn't do YTH ministry any different than I did 36 years ago. I would still major on prayer, worship, preaching, and evangelism. I don't believe these things have aged out of their usefulness in Christianity or the YTH culture.*

The Moderation of Re-invention

Let me explain the concept of "static success". Especially as it relates to religion and Christianity. In Hebrews 13, Paul said of Jesus, *"Christ is the same yesterday, today, and forever."* That would be the perfect illustration of "static success". It is the fact that some things will never require change at its concept level. It is also called "the moderation of reinvention".

It is the idea that some things do not require much change or altering at its DNA. Another concept related to this is called "evolved engineering". These similar concepts define the idea that the reinvention or the evolving of certain things will never need to happen. That there is such a thing as inventive or engineering "static success."

Those things will often be quite clear.

For example, there is no need to change the concept of the wheel – round is best. There is no need to change the concept of the pencil – lead works best and so do flat edges on the pencil barrel. The basic rules of a sport will never change – there will always be three bases and a plate in baseball. Finally, one thing that has withstood the test of time is time. The concept of time will never change.

What I have found interesting in YTH ministry, is that it has almost become a badge of honor to change for change sake. But the one thing that must remain unchanged in YTH ministry is to make disciples. I do not believe we can make disciples if we fail to teach students how to pray, worship, read their bible, and share their faith. Whatever else we are doing must yield to these things. Or we need to stop doing them.

You have heard it said before, if we continue to do the things that we are doing, we will continue to get the things that we have. The definition of insanity is doing the same thing over and over and expecting a different result. If we define most of YTH ministry today in America, it fits this insanity definition too well.

We have been doing too many things in YTH ministry the same way and expecting a different result. At some point we have to stop this fast moving train from continuing in this direction or we are going to get further and further away from our responsibility of the raw emphasis of discipleship through prayer, worship, preaching, and evangelism. This is what I believe classic YTH ministry values the most. I know some will disagree on how to get there. But what is obvious is that our approach needs to change because it's not working.

The millennial and the Gen Z sets are not completely familiar with the language or the atmosphere around such global religious Awakening or revival movements that took place in this classic YTH ministry era. Why do I believe this is true? Because the majority of our students are not in weekly prayer meetings, there is little elongated worship of Christ in YTH ministry, teenagers do not have a theology, and students are not taking to the streets or their world with sound apologetics and sharing their faith. These are the kind of things we saw in the classic YTH ministry era in the first 150 years of YTH ministry history, and they are missing in the church today.

And yet, undeniably, there are a few things about classic YTH ministry that have been showing signs of resuscitation in the coming years. Even if only in a few places. That has brought me and others great anticipation and optimism for the future of YTH ministry.

Social cycles will often reappear within a generation or two. If you look at where we are at in the millennial YTH ministry setting today, the classic YTH ministry model could be an approaching storm on the horizon. Do you see the correlation? Classic YTH ministry brought these four emphases of prayer, worship, preaching, and evangelism to the church. The cycle of the classic model of YTH ministry, with an emphasis on presence-based methods like we have seen in the past, could be the healthy difference in our YTH ministry future.

My Personal Experience

For example, I grew up in a YTH ministry in the 1970s that basically included acoustic worship, my YTH pastor preaching or teaching to us, and a prayer time at the end. Much of YTH ministry was done this way. What I remember most of my YTH ministry is that we were challenged to reach our world for Christ. I don't remember ever playing games or the need for creative attractional ideas. I think you have heard me say before, I have never played a game in YTH ministry, and yet we never struggled to draw a crowd of teenagers.

There was a major discipleship emphasis of small groups and Sunday School in the Classic setting. Who could forget their Sunday School days with the seventh grade boys in the basement classroom?! I knew all of the important characters in the Bible. This is where I learned the bigger than life stories of Moses, Noah, Joshua, Esther, David, Daniel, Mary, the Disciples, all of the miracles of Jesus, and how Christ would return again in the Rapture of the church.

But the small groups we see in YTH ministry today are not the same. Most of these small groups have turned into relational self-help discussions about everyday life. Sans theology, prayer, worship, and students coming to Christ.

Could it be the loss of the Classic approach to YTH ministry has been reason for the many negative statistics amongst teenagers? With this lack of the Classic YTH ministry model in the Millennial era, we have part of the cause why there is such a decline in the biblical worldview over the last two social sets. From percentages in the mid 30% for Gen X, in the teen percentage for millennials, and now the all-time low of 4% in Gen Z. (3)

> *And frankly, since these early days of classic YTH ministry, the YTH ministry numbers have not changed in 40 years. That is interesting to me. That no matter the era or the model or the budget or the creativity or even the growth in the number of churches, there really are not many more students involved in our YTH ministry nationwide as there were 4 decades ago.*

Looking at this older classic YTH ministry setting will help us to see more clearly some of the characteristics and trends and how they play into the future of YTH ministry. I know some of our younger readers will advocate for doing YTH ministry completely different – by bringing sweeping changes such as attractional methods, less large group meetings, highly discussive small groups, and watered down content in everything we do. This is exactly what many have been doing for the last two decades and we are living with the results.

We must take another look before we can accurately predict the future of YTH ministry. That look would be at YTH ministry in the most recent Millennial Age of YTH ministry in the last 20 years.

Millennial Age of YTH Ministry

The Millennial Age of YTH ministry today in the 21st-century is a completely different kind of methodology. In my estimation there are three streams within the Millennial age of YTH ministry. These approaches are described as they place their focus and each will venture into another approach, but, focus generally on their own methodology:

1. *A program-based graded age-stage (catechism)* philosophy with a focus upon small groups and activities
2. *A large group social presentation (gathering)* philosophy that is more social and hype-based
3. *A presence-based (responsive)* methodology that is a mix of the first two approaches to YTH ministry

Although there are many styles and kinds of YTH ministries represented in our nation, generally, YTH ministry in the last 20 years in America falls into one of these three settings.

What do these look like specifically? Parenthetically, there is a more in-depth training for these models coming in the following ythology books. But, let's take a skinny look at these models and see how each might lead us to a more definitive look at the future of YTH ministry.

Program-based and Age-stage-based Catechism YTH Ministry

This popular approach in YTH ministry will split the Junior High and the Senior High students into small group discussions rather than experiential services. This approach mimics the old model of Sunday School in the Classic era in that it leans toward relationships and games and dialogue and discipleship. Students are familiar with this because this is like the 6-7 hours they are in school daily (minus the games).

There are strengths and weaknesses to this of course.

Let me give you just a few for each.

Strengths of this model:

- The dire need for theology in this generation can be passed on to students in this setting in a special catechism-type way. With students demonstrating such a lack of spiritual formation, this model can bring a focus on doctrine and discipleship.
- This model gives leaders the chance to dialogue with students and build relationship and accountability if the groups are run well. Students can get relational conversation and comprehensive doctrine in the small group if the groups are run well.
- When students are in this setting with other peers this can be an explosive incubator for challenging and questioning their faith as they realize they are not alone in their pursuit of Christ.

Weaknesses of this model include:

- Poor leadership in the small group setting. On a regular basis I have watched small group leaders spend 75-80% of the time talking and students are listening (sometimes) rather than in dialogue that is critical for this model to work.
- Another weakness of this model of YTH ministry happens because of the lack of diversity when older mature students are not in with the younger students, or, if the groups are gender-based. Diversity and maturity is a great teacher. And it is much better to error on the side of expecting more out of Junior High students rather than slowing their growth with juvenialization or isolation.
- Maybe the most notable weakness of this model is the lack of presence and the operation of the gifts of the Holy Spirit in setting. This setting does not normally allow for the moving of the Spirit and the presence of God. And if this is not happening in the weekend services in the adult setting, where will the students learn the benefits of the working of the Spirit and His presence?

I am not saying that *programming* and *graded age-stage catechism* ministry is not important. I am not saying that organization and administration and structure is not spiritual. We need discipleship and systems and organization. I am not saying we don't need graded or aged discipleship in YTH ministry. I am not saying students do not want to play games.

Although, I hear many students say to me the games they are playing are boring, unorganized, and a waste of time. *Graded age-stage* ministry is important to a holistic YTH ministry when it is done right.

Presentation or Gathering-based Social YTH Ministry

This is another popular approach of YTH ministry in modern America.

In this present age of YTH ministry there is a major emphasis upon *presentation* and *gathering*. Largely hype-based gatherings that evaluate their meetings or services with statements like, "Did we have a good time?" or, "The speaker was on fire!" or, "What was the attendance?" There is a major emphasis upon presentation and delivery and excitement and there is less of an emphasis upon presence and response. Attending the *after-party* can actually become more important than living the *after-life*.

With the emphasis of presentation rather than response, this YTH ministry approach can become more like inspirational rallies than transformational rallies. And in the end, they are promoted with exciting photos, talking points, and quip videos on social platforms.

Let me give you a few weaknesses and strengths of this model.

Weaknesses of this model:

- There is a greater emphasis upon gathering and culture-building than going and disciple-making. The service, rally, convention, or event is the highlight and there is little emphasis upon taking the moment public. It may be those attending haven't read their bible, prayed, or worshipped since the last time they gathered in a service.
- This approach can become personality driven and ego-stroking for those involved from the fanfare and following that takes place in this setting. It can be easy to love crowds but not people. Or, to love the crowds more than the Christ. The danger here is that we measure ourselves by the presentation and not by the transformation.

- Most of the time this setting will lack a response or application, even in the moment, as well as after the event or gathering, as the goal is often presentation and not response. Because of the hype or focus of this approach, there can be little repentance, brokenness, accountability, relationship, or depth in a transformational way.

Strengths of this model:

- Great moments can be made out of preparation and expectation. Suddenlies in this setting can bring instant change that lasts a lifetime. Never under-estimate what God can do in a moment.
- This setting can be very attractional for an a/v based generation moved by attractional energy. It is settings like this that can attract an unchurched crowd and be an introduction into the deeper things of the church.
- Inspirational settings like this can get a negative reaction from the pragmatic crowd. But with a more inspirational and deeper faith emphasis, there can be a moment of accountability in this setting if it is led by leadership who value transformation. And the gathering can lead to going and apologetics if it is intentional.

I'm sure you understand these are generalist statements from my broad experiences over 4 decades of seeing all kinds of YTH settings across this nation. Like always, every setting will rise and fall on leadership. I have seen both of these settings escape the stereotype and balance the methods to gain the right outcomes and be very healthy.

So what should we be looking for in the future of YTH ministry? Let me give you a compilation of the three – a *programming-based, a presentation-based,* and finally, a *presence-based* YTH setting.

Presence-based YTH Ministry

This setting can be most like the first 150 years of YTH ministry in the classic sense, and yet, most like the *programming* and *presentation*-based ministries. Taking the theology of the small group setting and the excellence of the large group production and marrying it with a responsive YTH ministry setting. Because most of the Millennial Age ministries today will swing the pendulum between the *graded* or *gathering* type of models, a *presence-based* model can be a unique compilation of both. Why is this so?

First, thinking about the *program* or *graded* approach, our students do not always connect in the adult weekend services of churches because they don't attend, or, because the currency of the adult services does not appeal to them, or, the YTH small group is poorly done. This results in students not getting a corporate worship setting that is presence-based. This can be stunting to their spiritual formation.

Second, thinking about the *presentation* approach, if our YTH ministry does not get students to the doctrine and the faith in His presence, they will not experience the lasting power of this corporate moment. It is not enough to be in His presence without response. Our students must sense the depth of a corporate moment as leaders place value on this setting with as much relational response as they can guide. And the result should be apologetics.

Third, the *presence-based* approach may not be happening in a viral sense, but YTH ministries across the country who are emphasizing a *presence-based* ministry are, I believe, seeing a return to the classic era of YTH ministry. A setting with a *heightened spiritual discipline* we have not seen in this generation. It is doctrinally sound and transformative. This *presence*-based setting has an expectation of response. It values truth on fire. There is both a theology and a theatre to the moment that produces both information and inspiration, truth and transformation, and programming and presence.

Weaknesses of this model:

- If we are not careful, the presence-based model can become rote and familiar. It will begin to lack mystery and creativity and can lead to meaningless practice.
- One of the dangers of this model happens when we become too religious in our response and language so an unchurched crowd would not be interested in the setting. Leaders in this setting must guard familiarity by leading with a variety of order.
- Finally, in this setting it can be easy to revert to learned responses to the Spirit. If something doesn't happen a certain way it is not accepted. When we lose the Word and theology and the Spirit in any of these settings, we lose the spiritual approach.

Strengths of this model:

- The setting values response and not simply rehearsal. The leaders in this setting make room for involvement and do not settle for spectatorship. Time is given for students to grow in their discernment and experience of God personally. Beyond the moment.
- There is a focused effort on *internal attendance* that seeks to get everyone to *external influence*. Not just gathering in His presence, but, going with His presence.
- Jesus proved this *presence*-based approach could share both the small group relational capital and the large group inspirational capital. He did that in the feeding of the 4,000 and the 5,000 as He did both the teaching and the meal in one setting.
- One of the strengths of this approach is the diversity in the crowd. This diversity can bring a university of influence as we are with others and experience their relationship with God. This becomes true community ministry as Paul described it in Corinthians, "One brings a hymn, one brings a psalm, and another a prophecy...."
- This model can bring the most people into the unity of the Spirit as they are all in the same setting and experience the presence of God. The attractional piece of this culture-setting rivals concerts or game atmospheres students will experience in other settings. But a *presence*-based YTH ministry has a big advantage. The presence of God.
- My favorite outcome of this setting is the experiential work of the Holy Spirit in the teens. Where there is focus and value placed upon the ministry of the Spirit, the gifts begin to operate in the students and the supernatural is introduced.

What is very true as I travel across the country, is that YTH ministry has struggled through the years to balance *programming, presentation, and presence*.

The *program*-based (*graded age-stage*-based) people want relationship and structure and discipleship and the teaching of God in a smaller setting. The *presentation* (*gathering*-based) people want hype and holiness and inspirational discipleship and the teaching of God in a larger setting. And the *presence*-based people want spiritual formation, relationship and the experience of discipleship, and the teaching of God in an interactive responsive setting.

> I don't believe the three need to be mutually exclusive. Programming can be spiritual and presence can be structured. Presentation can be relational and programming

can be inspirational. It just takes a lot of leadership to pull this off holistically in a YTH ministry. But I believe each model can be alive in the Spirit, and, create a biblically challenging and responsive teenager. However, I think you can sense my model of YTH ministry was guided by the third – a presence-based approach.

We cannot raise another generation void of theology, presence, and spiritual discipline. At this time in history, we have the greatest need for discipleship and a deepening of the faith of teenagers than ever before.

Our teenagers need to find a faith of their own in Christianity. The faith of their grandparents, parents, pastors, a camp or convention experience, or some podcast is not going to be sustainable when the cultural wave crashes upon them. I believe the Classic YTH ministry model shares the best of each of these *programming* and *presentation*-based approaches.

Why is this?

Because I do not believe a completely *programming*-based or a completely *presentation*-based YTH ministry is the answer for the future of YTH ministry. The most comprehensive and biblical YTH ministry I see is founded in the few principles that guided Classic YTH ministry and its evolution and resurfacing. With a little effort and application from both the *programming* and the *presentation* people, this return to Classic YTH ministry could spark the best of times for the future of YTH ministry.

So, with that quick review in mind, here are 7 futurist ethics or commitments I believe must be part of YTH ministry in the next 50 years. If the Lord tarries.

Five Ethics for the Future of YTH Ministry:

Contextual YTH Ethic

Here's the problem. The average codependent student in the average YTH ministry in America doesn't read their bible in their bedroom, hasn't worshipped in their free time, or wouldn't know how to share their faith in the teenage context if they had to save their life.

To change this, we must raise student converts into student disciples who would rather be the church than simply just go to church. We must get students to understand they can serve God in the context of their own world.

What does that context look like?

Lynn Browne, a co-founder of BrandVerge, a marketing company that focuses upon digital natives, defines the teenage context simplistically this way.

> *"They are digital natives, global, and have big dreams. One hallmark of Gen Z is they are the first generation to grow up with the Internet. Thanks to that exposure, they are also the first global generation. They are also entrepreneurial; 76 percent of Gen Z say they want to be a founder. Twenty-four percent are online "almost constantly," and are defined by their tech use and a desire to stand out. This generation also prefers to spend money on experiences over products, and the products they do choose must be "unique" – becoming an experience in and of themselves." (4)*

The teen context can be found in sectors such as the family, their schools, their teams, and in the places where they hang out like malls, skate parks, a friend's house, and theatres. A missional mindset of every future YTH leader must be to be present in these settings and sectors of students and teenagers. It has been said many times, most of success is simply showing up. God is present in all things in and outside of the church building! We must meet students at the local well – their contextual hangout.

YTH Ministry in America cannot solely highlight serving God in the confines of the church. It must get to context – in the neutral setting of where students live. We have secluded our work to the church property and thus have created codependent teenagers who haven't seen their faith outside of the church setting. They haven't worshipped, read their bible, or shared their faith with anyone outside of church since the last time they went to YTH group. YTH ministry needs a re-introduction to the teen world.

What does that look like practically?

YTH leaders who are doing ministry in context will be frequent visitors and have involvement in the following settings: in the *community* setting at events such as sporting activities, theatre, malls, coffee shops, fairs, carnivals, concerts, and skate parks. In the *school* setting with on campus allowances such as counseling, substitute teaching, coaching, and lunch room monitoring. The school campus setting would also include extra-curricular activities such as sports, theatre, band/chorale, and other competitions like DECA, clubs, and debate.

YTH leaders who develop a contextual ethic will not make excuses for themselves about being in the YTH setting – they will make solutions. A return to the streets where YTH ministry began through Sunday School outreach would be a great idea for the future of YTH ministry.

Neutral-site Ethic

Similar to the previous ethic, this is where the future of YTH ministry itself must be more than a gathering. Not just YTH leaders, but, the whole of YTH ministry. It must be an apologetic going and it must take place in neutral-site settings. Similar to the contextual ethic, this ethic will require YTH leaders, and not just our students, being in context also.

Every YTH leader and YTH ministry must become a sociologist and a sociological movement understanding culture and subculture. This will make YTH ministry more public and will create missional students. After all, 71% of Gen Z would go to church if asked.

> *Remember, more miracles happened in the bible outside of the temple. Just in Mark 1-6 there are about 26 works of Jesus among the people - and only 2 of those took place in the temple or the synagogue. That is astounding. Because we operate the opposite of this today. We have created a generation of teenagers who are co-dependent upon the safety of the church building or the YTH service to practice their faith. A generation who equates serving God with going to church.*

Too often in this generation, YTH Ministry is raising codependent students. Let me explain. The YTH group becomes the place they go to be spiritual. But their faith never gets to the other sectors of their life - their home, their school, their workplace, their team, or their friends. Someone asked me one time how to balance the Christian life. I know what they are saying – how to balance family, or time management, or even my emotions and wellness. But the best way to answer this is to say the Christian life is not about balance – it is about centrality. Keeping Christ at the center of everything and not allowing anything to be out from under His influence. It is when our students break from this centrality they are not independently Christian. Hey are co-dependently Christian.

What does that look like practically?

Something as simple as having YTH services and events every quarter outside of the church building and in the community. This can take the students public in their faith. We must also make sure our outreaches are not solely held at the church building. It makes sense to do evangelism in the community where the target lives. Another discipline in YTH ministry is having YTH leaders who are recognizable in multiple settings outside of the church (school, para-church, government, and the community).

We have to retrain students that the faith of the church is for the fears of the world. To model to our students that we do not simply go to church. We are the church.

The Diversity Ethic

There is a growing movement in this present generation we have not seen. Ever. Gen Z is the largest non-white generation in American history. At this point 51% of Gen Z is non-white. That is historical and this trait must shape the way we do YTH ministry in the next 50 years. If the Lord tarries, we could be on the verge of re-writing the race relations narrative in the church and ultimately in the culture if we continue with this healing and diversity trend.

> *The growing gracism in this generation is undeniable. This diversity narrative will be either a success or a failure dependent upon the YTH leaders of the church who teach new language and terms and who demonstrate race ethic actions.*

Every time we speak of the past sins of our nation, YTH leaders must speak too of the beauty of gracism growing in the young people of our nation. Simply look at my Instagram over the past three months. My social media has become a clear depiction of the growing diversity in the Church. Look at their respect. See the joy. Hear the laughter. Feel the love. See the social media of so many YTH leaders across our country. It's undeniable. We are on the verge of our "one day" as MLK, Jr. said!

The growing gracism in our nation must be allowed to re-write the narrative of racism at some time in America's history. Gracism must be an accompanied chapter in every writing on race relations. Gracism must be the spoken word in every conversation on race relations. And gracism must be the common good in our fight against the evil of racism. What we celebrate we are going to get. So let's celebrate this growing diversity in Gen Z and place the pen in their capable hands and help them write the new narrative of race relations in America.

What does that look like practically?

Make sure the make-up of your leadership team reflects your diversity valuation. We must open our circles or tribes or squads and be more inclusive in our friendships. Are we leading *intentional* and *tensional* effort through our language and programming that is sensitive to minority groups who exist in the community of your reach?

As YTH leaders, our leadership should include intentionally diverse leadership teams, use of restorative language, encouraging adult and student leaders to sit and friend outside of their racial circles, YTH leaders should learn basic Spanish, and including various racial illustrations for sermons and messaging.

These practical preparations are important. But foremost in this effort of leading YTH ministries in diversity valuation is for white people to lead the way and repent of racism and prejudice. And for all people to follow and repent of their own indigenous racism and prejudice. This is not a mono-problem or does it have a mono-solution. As I am witnessing this gracism in Gen Z across our nation, it is emotionally moving and deeply healing for all. If we let it rise.

A Theology Ethic

Another Gen Z trait that should influence the future of YTH ministry is that only 4% of this generation has a Biblical worldview. This demands YTH leaders are prepared theologically themselves and have a stepped plan for increasing biblical knowledge in teenagers annually. Also included in this needed ethic is that Atheism is at its highest percentage than any generation. It cannot be a very encouraging trend that we have created more atheists than any time in American history.

We must see a renewed emphasis on theology in YTH ministry.

I want to say something at the outset of this ethic. Forgive my rant, but, you have the book so you might as well read this! Ha.

> *I hear so many leaders say they don't preach. That this generation is turned off to preaching and they won't respond to it. They want to have conversations. Really? So, we are gonna listen to culture and sociological approaches that have produced the failing statistical information about spirituality in Gen Z today? I think this is a cop out. An excuse to not work hard at the art of preaching.*
>
> *I'm not saying throw out conversations and small groups.*
>
> *What I'm saying is there is great theology and discipleship in preaching. It is throughout scripture. There is a place for the rabbi, mentoring, small group, and worship in discipleship. But, biblical preaching is a great way to disciple your students in theology also.*

This was covered extensively in chapter 2 so we will not take much time here.

Roller Coasters and Preachers on Fire

The importance of theology and its relationship with discipleship is inseparable. I believe it is desirable in this Millennial and Gen Z set because of their lack of the knowledge of God. This lack of knowledge is a setup for attraction. Instead of shying away from theology thinking this generational set is not interested, why not introduce a theology on fire to this generation?

> *Remember, what you get teenagers with, you have to keep them with. Building a YTH ministry on theology is an exploration of never ending creativity and wonder. But building a YTH ministry on the latest program and event or game can become stale and familiar. Roller coasters do attract teens, but, students become familiar with these. Besides, it is very expensive to build a new roller coaster every year to attract teens. Just ask Disney or Great America, or Cedar Point.*

Back in the day we used to have this saying. It went something like this:
Set yourself on fire and people will come from hours to watch you burn for days.

That probably brings to mind a house fire or an ambulance chase or an accident on the highway. Those kind of things get our attention and turn our heads. One of the most important principles to keep in mind with theology in YTH ministry is that it will require YTH leaders to become biblical in their own lives as they lead their ministry. In a sense, to light themselves on fire for all to see. There is still a lot of truth in this age old saying about classic preachers.

What does that look like practically?

YTH ministry needs leaders who are on fire – or lit as they say. YTH ministry needs leaders who students want to emulate. Students need leaders who are iconic in a spiritual sense.

We cannot shy away from emphatic biblical teaching and preaching of theology, language and term definition, and a basic understanding of key Christian concepts. As we talked about earlier in chapter 2, this would include The 10 Commandments, Proverbs, the Sermon on the Mount, the Trinity, the gifts/fruit of the Spirit, sanctification and justification, apologetics, and eschatology. Every student who leaves our YTH ministry should have a basic understanding of these things.

Another important tool for growing theology in your YTH ministry is to look at the songs you are singing and make sure there is good theology in each. This is a great way to disciple students. Music is central to their lives and the world they live in so we must redeem music in YTH ministry. If the emphasis upon theology is done systematically, we will decrease the number of students who are leaving the church in the transition years after high school and right before and during college.

When every student graduates out of the YTH ministry they must have a certain set of principles. Do you have those non-negotiable principles of YTH ministry? If you can create these, they will become the measurement and the assessment of whether your YTH ministry is successful or not. A new theology ethic is clearly a must for the future of YTH ministry because we cannot continue the trends of raising a biblically illiterate generation.

The Sexuality Ethic
This will be itemized and dealt with in more detail in the following book on YTH & Sexuality coming out in 2020.

The Sexual Revolution going on in America is redefining how the world views family, marriage, sexuality, and gender. With the redefinition of once held conservative standard values, there is a lot of confusion surrounding the family, marriage, sexuality, and gender. For instance, the family has been disintegrated in America, marriage has been redefined by government, students are having sex at an earlier age, and at last count there were more than 30 gender type names that have been created just in the past couple of years.

Here are a few of those terms in an abbreviated list:

Androsexual: Being sexually, aesthetically, and/or romantically attracted to masculinity

Aromantic: Experiences little or no romantic attraction to others

Bigender: People who feel they have both a male and female side

Cisgender: Gender identity matches the sex they were assigned at birth

Demiromantic: People who do not experience romantic attraction until a strong emotional or sexual connection is formed with a partner

Gender binary/Non-binary: The idea that there are only two distinct and different genders: Female/Male. And, that there are many and not exclusive of Female/Male.

Gender Fluidity: Gender identity varies over time and changes at will

Intersex: Biologically neither completely male nor completely female

Panromantic: Romantically attracted – but not sexually attracted – to others regardless of gender

Polysexual: Attracted to multiple genders while rejecting the idea that there are only two genders (male and female).

Queer: An adjective used by some people, particularly younger people, for those who only identify as queer, because the terms lesbian, gay, and bisexual are perceived to be too limiting

It is stunning to see the variety of ways culture and people define their sexuality since things have changed from our standardized understanding of the biblical intent of the creation of male and female. Because teenagers predominantly get their sexual identity definition from culture and their peers, YTH ministry is going to have to become a voice that defines a biblical and human sexual identity for teenagers amidst the 21st century Sexual Revolution.

This ethic will require YTH leaders have an understanding of both the cultural influences and the biblical theology of human sexuality. Understanding *cultural* influences such as progressive ideology in pop music, movies, and their peers, and, understanding *biblical* theology such as the creation intent of Moses in the Old Testament, as well as, the Messianic intent of Jesus and Paul in the New Testament.

Critical to adolescent sexual development is determining where teens are acquiring both the theory and the practice of a sexual ethic. If not the home or the church, where will teenagers get their sexuality principles? Where will they get the practical training it takes to protect their sexuality principles? I believe because the family has failed largely at this, it must be YTH ministry across our nation who will help families educate their children on biblical sexual identity. Which in turn will counter the cultural impact happening on sexuality in their schools, on their screens, and amongst their peers.

What does that look like practically?

Okay, so we have a different interpretation of sexuality in the scriptures than some people may have. Maybe you believe, as I have stated in this book, that marriage is between a man and a woman, that sex before marriage, outside of marriage, or with the same sex is not God's intent, and that God created humanity male and female. But just because someone believes differently than we do, what right does that give us to treat them with partiality or judgement?

The anger on all sides of this topic simply stems from a lack of respect for the person and an overemphasis on the issue.

In a perfect world, one of the priorities of YTH ministry in the Sexual Revolution era is to walk in both disciplined and intentional truth and grace – in both regulation and relationship. We do not have to shed our principles at the door of a progressive society. But we cannot become judgmental or cynical and burn the house down either.

> *A part of this sexual ethic as YTH leaders is the truthful and gracious reaction to the unbiblical lifestyles around us. Truth and grace work together. Our reaction to the sin of this world will determine the world's reaction to the grace of the church. We cannot blush in the face of a new age of sexuality. We must smile and look them in the eye and love them. And then tell them the truth.*

Gen Z and the next generation to come, whatever we will call them, have the opportunity to be the comeback generation! How? By redefining sexuality, the leading issue in their culture, with a biblical view of sexuality. By facing one of the biggest issues in their generation and resetting it publicly according to scripture. This is the critical role we play as YTH leaders in preparing this younger generation to face their world and its sexuality issues with apologetic confidence.

One of the things YTH leaders must model to their ministry is that people do not have to behave to belong. People must be welcomed before justification and they must be loved until sanctification. The spiritual comeback we are looking for in society is going to have to begin now and with our young people – the statistics cannot get any lower.

*Again, we will delve into detail on this topic in the next release in 2020.

Student Leadership Development Ethic

Another critical ethic that must become a foundational principle of future YTH ministry is the leadership development of students. A YTH group should be a leadership factory. Why?

In most sociological studies, a key characteristic trait of the present Millennial and Gen Z set is achievement and competition.

Teenagers have leadership born within them. But we must move beyond **natural** leadership development like communication, social skills, time management, and cultural understanding – and focus as well on the **spiritual** leadership development like integrity, spiritual disciplines, and scriptural understanding. We are leading the next leaders of the church and that is a great responsibility.

Look at the desk or the bookshelf or the Kindle app of most YTH leaders and you will see the growth we need in this area. Most YTH leaders will have system-type leadership books – management systems, the team dynamics, operational advantage, personality and gift assessment testing, and marketing and advertising plans. They are focused highly upon personality, culture, and organizational leadership development more than theology, integrity, and personal spiritual leadership development. I think it is clear to all of us we need both/and.

Student and adult leaders in a YTH ministry can be a firework display of spiritual growth in their generation!

We are not going to convince teenagers to become passionate and hungry for God if we as YTH leaders and our student and adult leaders are not passionate and hungry for God. We must explosively model the spiritual disciplines (prayer, bible reading, worship, giving, fasting, simplicity, etc.) consistently to them. They are watching. Our lives are the gateway to a dynamic Christian life for those who are around us. The millennial and the Gen Z set need spiritual icons, both adult and peer, they can look up to and to whom they are attracted.

What does that look like practically?

One of the *personal* ways we can increase student leadership development as YTH leaders is through our example. We may be the only mature Christian some of our students ever see. So, what do they see? Do they sense our relationship with God because we are praying? Do they see us reading the Bible? Do they hear us abandoned in worship? Do they witness us sharing our faith? Have they experienced our giving? How about our personal spiritual and natural leadership development?

One of the *corporate* ways we can increase student leadership development as YTH leaders is through regular leadership development that is intentional and comprehensive. When a YTH leader plans leadership meetings that are a value-add to the teens, the meetings will be enthusiastically attended. Another corporate leadership increase is annual YTH leadership weekends or conferences for intensive leadership training. These are great settings where lids can be taken off and fences can be removed so students can run in their natural leadership field!

Spiritually healthy YTH student leaders produce spiritually healthy YTH ministry.

A Volunteer Movement Ethic

The future of YTH ministry will be impacted greatly by volunteers. One of the noted realities of this modern Millennial-age of YTH ministry is the number of volunteer YTH leaders in America. Volunteer leaders in YTH ministry overwhelmingly outnumber full-time YTH pastors.

But here is the reality. The data is very difficult to find and even more difficult to trust. At the time of this book publication, if you Googled "volunteer youth pastor" you would see over 32 million results. On the other hand, if you Googled "full time youth pastor" you would see 21.3 million results. Now I know this is not scientific. But I think it has a lot to do with my point. I just randomly did that while writing the book.

I do believe this elementary Google search is indicative of the exhaustive nature of volunteer YTH ministry.

I want to give you specific research from my denomination coupled with findings from several of the other larger denominations. These are percentages and numbers of paid and part-time YTH leaders. For many of you it will be understandable, but, for some the findings will be hard to believe.

Here are the percentage of churches in the Assemblies of God who have reported a paid YTH leader (full or part-time). This is information gathered from the Annual Church Ministry Report (ACMR):

2010 - 25.2%
2011 - 24.6%
2012 - 23.8%
2013 - 23.5%
2014 - 23.2%
2015 - 22.7%
2016 - 22.5%
2017 - 22.1%

Here are some more statistics from our denomination from our Annual Church Ministry Report (ACMR). These are the number of churches annually who reported a paid YTH leader (full or part-time):

2010 – 3,143
2011 – 3,105
2012 – 3,030
2013 – 3,017
2014 – 2,989
2015 – 2,933
2016 – 2,930
2017 – 2,879

It is obvious in this ACMR report that the statistics for YTH leadership in the church have gone down since 2010 in both categories. What has increased also is the number of churches we have in the U.S. – about 13,000. The church planting movement has increased this by about 2,500 churches in the last decade. But what is disheartening is that YTH ministry has not grown in emphasis – it has actually shrunk every year during the last decade.

What is obvious from this report is the high majority of YTH ministry in U.S. churches that are led by non-paid YTH volunteers. If we do not raise the level of the volunteer leader in YTH ministry, we do not raise the level of YTH ministry in America. A deeper dive into this reality will show further that we need a YTH ministry ethic to be at the heart of senior ministry leaders in the church.

It has become clear that YTH ministry is not a priority in the church today and this must change.

The Supernatural Ethic

The final ethic or discipline that must become a foundation in futurist YTH ministry is the supernatural signs and wonders of the Kingdom.

One thing we have learned from this generation is their love of the supernatural. It is in their movies, music, reading, and our culture. In order for YTH ministry to see students take their faith into neutral settings and to live their faith outside of the church, they must see God is present with them. Always. The supernatural aspect of the Trinity is alluring to teenagers and that is specifically the role of the Holy Spirit in our lives. There is an obvious lack of understanding of who the Holy Spirit is and how He works in our lives. By defining this better to teenagers we can attract them to a powerful relationship with the Holy Spirit.

> We must emphasize the supernatural relationship of the Holy Spirit with teenagers. As YTH leaders it is our responsibility to create this setting. The local YTH ministry must be placed back in the hands of Holy Spirit led teenagers who can lead the church to its greatest days.

All throughout scripture moments turned into movements because of the Holy Spirit's work in someone's life. When Jesus ascended, He placed a major emphasis upon the role of the Holy Spirit in our lives. The Holy Spirit would bring us power, conviction, truth, and help with gifts in our time of need. Some of the most mature young teenagers in my ministry over the years have had a great relationship with the Holy Spirit and they have demonstrated power to live for Christ because of it.

The Next (Third) Great Awakening will require spiritual principles that must be taught to this generation. But make no mistake about it. Some things are taught and some things are caught. Given the state of our country, and the approaches of the last 50 years in YTH ministry, we need help. We need a supernatural move of God upon the church that will impact culture as we have never seen. The church and YTH ministry must regain their voice again.

Just a few years ago, one of the unique traits of our country's DNA was challenged from the top of our nation's leadership. President Obama stated in 2010, "America is no longer a Christian nation..." Now, please don't go political on me right now. He may have been more right in saying this than wrong. But, we must understand that from the top of our nation's leadership, in that moment, we lost the profession of the founding principles that were so evident in our beginnings. That we are making this statement at such a high level is testament to our demise as a nation.

I get the context from President Obama's quote – that we are now Jewish, Muslim, Hindu, and pagan (or unbelieving). But, just because our nation has become diverse religiously and culturally, doesn't mean we must become divisible from our scriptural Christian foundations. You can see in our nation in this moment the drift from civil behavior let alone Christian behavior.

What this presidential quote revealed many years ago is the vacuum in our country and our missing spiritual virtues. Look, for example, at something as simple as our elected official's relationships. America has become an angry nation revealed in a bullying culture displayed at the top of our nation's leadership. But it really doesn't stop there because social media has revealed it also.

It is difficult to shape adolescents to become peacemakers in our angry society when social media and our leaders display bullying behavior to one another in the very public sector. All this simply proves is that, because of this spiritual vacuum, the teenage generation has a chance to bring in the next great move of God.

Finally: The Impact of Teenagers on the Future of YTH Ministry

As we close out this book, I want to remind you of an important looming fact.

We don't have to look far to see the impact of teenagers on a society. Teenagers like Alexander the Great (who conquered his first colony in 4th century Persia at 16), Joan of Arc (the 13 year old French revolutionary in the 15th century), Louis Braille (inventing language to the blind in the 19th century at age 15), Mozart completing an opera at 14, or even our contemporaries Mark Zuckerberg and Bill Gates who both took their companies public by creating Facebook and Microsoft at the age of 19.

Look at the number of teenagers who gained an overnight following on social media and in the public conversation after the shootings at Stoneman-Douglas High School in Florida. Several of these teenagers became viral influencers and shifted the thinking and the action toward gun control in our country in a matter of days.

> *I believe teenagers in America are not done writing their narrative for our culture. I know there are more dreams to be dreamt. I have no doubt there are more songs, and poems, and books to be written. With everything in me I am convinced there are companies and businesses yet to be born. And revivals and awakenings yet to be led.*

What only remains to be seen is who will be the YTH leaders in America today that will step into leadership roles to equip these young teenagers? Who will be the YTH leaders in America that will be in proximity of these teenagers and pull the stories, dreams, songs, poems, books, and businesses out of this generation? Will the church position itself to speak into the teenagers who will shape the future of our country?

Needless to say, we may be witnessing another civil and religious surge in America right now. In part because of the lowly depths we have reached in America as we look at issues like human-trafficking, opioid epidemic, the sexual revolution, disunity in government, racial tension in adults, school shootings, and the disintegration of the family.

These kinds of things tend to have a negative effect upon society and can be cause for either a civil and religious surge or decline.

Because of this, I believe we are in the beginning stages of a civil and religious surge that is already being ushered in through the young people of our nation as they are praying underground and going public for *The Next (third) Great Awakening*.

9/11

Remember the 6 months after the 9/11 tragedy? The unity in America was breathtaking as we watched our government leaders on the steps of the Capitol building singing together. Every night we saw stories on the news of the survivors and the slain that was both inspirational and overwhelming. The resurgence in the attendance at our Churches from the deep pain felt became one of the great moments of our religious lives in America. The outcome of the 9/11 attacks has been relative safety and national security for the last two decades.

Unfortunately, the civil and the religious Awakening didn't last. Because just a few months after this surge in patriotism and religious excitement, everything went back to normal. It is a verified and published fact, for instance, that the sizable attendance increase in Church attendance post 9/11 was right back to normal by March 2002.

But, let's hope things are different this time.

I believe we are going to see another civil and religious surge in America rise out of all of these national economic and political and religious crises. And I believe the young people of the church are going to lead this resurgence.

For instance, in the wake of the Donald Trump presidency, the post-Parkland shooting tragedy at Stoneman-Douglas High School, and the rise of diversity and Gracism around the country, teenagers have been thrust into the spotlight. In just these three highly publicized incidents, we are watching the political disunity that comes with a divided government, gun control debate, and racism. We are viewing these stories on the news as they develop right before our eyes. Teenagers became the object of events and the focus of our debates that included both heroism and unfortunate death.

Yet, in each of these significant events of teen life, arguably, we are seeing students take leadership in every sector of society again. Including government, education, entertainment, athletics, social media, and The White House.

Beyond society, the church has been affected by teenagers before and it will again. Just look at the revivals in the YTH ministry history in chapter one. I believe today in 2019 our nation will once again have to focus upon teenagers and their rise to help shift the church and society. I believe 2025 will prove YTH ministry in America was at the forefront of an Awakening. What is undeniable, is we are in the beginnings of a post-crisis moment in our nation once again. I believe our nation's YTH will help to lead us to another civil and religious revival in the church and an Awakening in society.

As in many of the Awakenings detailed in this chapter, often times a spiritual desperation comes from a spiritual depletion. Looking at what's going on in America, we are poised for the greatest Awakening in the history of our country. Of that I am sure. But it will take some changes to the future of YTH ministry if we are going to see healthy YTH ministry lead the church and our nation to its greatest days.

Look at this thought from Purdue University sociology professor Fenggang Yang:

> "Adherents to Christianity, he said, have been increasing about 10 percent annually in China for nearly 40 years. Christianity is the dominant religion in the United States, the world's third most populous country, and Brazil, the fifth most populous. But China will be home to more Christians than these countries by 2030, Yang said. With 1.4 billion people, China's population, of course, dwarfs the U.S. population of 329 million.
>
> In Harris County, Asians made up 7 percent of the population in 2016, and 1 percent of the population speaks Chinese, according to the U.S. Census Bureau.
>
> Christianity is growing in China even though the government does not promote the faith, has closed churches, and jailed some believers. Exactly how many Chinese are Christian is difficult to estimate because some people will not reveal that they are Christians - they fear government reprisal, Yang said. In surveys, about 3 percent of

Chinese say they are Christian. Yang said the number is more likely at least 5 percent of the population."

Many other Chinese lost faith in Communist ideology when the government sent tanks into Tiananmen Square in 1989 and cracked down on student-led protesters seeking democratic reforms. And as the Chinese economy grew and the pace of modernization picked up, some Chinese have turned to religion. During rapid social change, people want something. Many people were looking for some religion, some alternative to communism, and they found it in Christianity." Yang said. (4)

A Wild Awakening in the Midst of a Raging Culture

One of the biggest changes that will need to take place, aside from these future ethics, will be this idea of laying aside our risk-aversion and bringing a wild Awakening to our raging culture. Do you see the impact a wild Awakening can have on a raging culture?

"During rapid social change", as Yang says, people are turning to something else for answers. Sometimes upheaval is what brings the shift and the change, and, Christ in the middle of the mess is what people are looking for. It is evident in China that all of the suppression actually brought an Awakening to Christianity.

In Professor Yang's case, the years after the Tiananmen Square protests, Yang, a former teacher of Marxist thought, said he stopped being an atheist and became a Christian while studying philosophy and earning his doctorate at Catholic University of America. No doubt all of this suppression had something to do with Yang's conversion.

Furthermore, Sunday Express, a British publication, reported in the summer of 1989 that the name of the protestor was Wang Weilin, a 19-year-old student arrested for "political hooliganism." Varying reports suggested the student was either imprisoned or executed. Chinese officials have refused to confirm his name or whereabouts in response to numerous queries from Western journalists in the years since the incident. In fact, they claim they were unable to locate him. (5)

Look at what happened in China in the months and years afterward. It took a wild Awakening to bring about the incredible change that happens in the midst of a raging culture.

I believe the future of YTH ministry will bring exactly what The Jesus Movement brought 50 years ago. In the aftermath of that movement America was shaken. I believe the future of YTH ministry will bring exactly what the lone protestor in Tiananmen Square brought to the Chinese communist government 30 years ago. In the aftermath of the incident, the lone protester who courageously stood in front of the Chinese tanks brought the focus to a China and he received worldwide fandom for his courage to challenge government oppression.

Revolutionary Righteousness and Love

There is something about a wild Awakening in the midst of a raging culture that will bring about change. A wild Awakening is exactly what we need again today out of YTH ministry in America. Looking at what is going on in our nation today, as the church we need another shift in our response to the suppression in our society. Young people in the church must rally and stand as a spiritual force against the tsunami of unrighteousness in our culture.

A wild Awakening could be defined as a radical commitment of young people to the spiritual disciplines of discipleship and Christianity. Not a revolution of radical protesting and angry mob tactics, but, a revolutionary righteousness and love that resets society with the life of Christ manifest in a new breed of teenagers. There is something about a wild Awakening in the midst of a raging culture. It matches the intensity of the evil with an intensity of good that overcomes the evil.

In world history, what the Trump presidency, the Stoneman-Douglas HS shooting, the rise of Gracism, and the Tiananmen Square standoff have shown us is that God has His Teenagers who are willing to take their cause to the White House, create a movement against violence, love their neighbors like themselves, and stand in front of tanks in the market place. I understand that not all of them may be Christian. But the potential in Gen Z for rising up for a cause is there and must be considered by YTH leaders today.

These kind of moments are what bring a tipping point of change to a society through radical and wild means. There is something about a wild Awakening in the midst of a raging culture.

This time in American history is an opportunity for a generation of teenagers to respond and to embrace Christianity and bring a sweeping Awakening to our nation. In the face of the current conditions in our nation, with more than 2.5 million engaged teenage Christians in our YTH ministries, we must make it our lifetime commitment as YTH leaders to raise the level of YTH ministry in America.

Because the future of the church and ultimately our nation depends upon it.

Action Steps

Questions Leading to Futurism

If we could predict the next phase of YTH ministry, what would it look like? Here are some questions to help you get there with your leadership team.

- *Could the future of YTH ministry become more housed or small group based? What would be the strengths and weaknesses of this?*
- *Will YTH ministry become more public and large group based? What would be the strengths and weaknesses of this?*
- *Can YTH ministry succeed in a neutral site setting like a school, a mall, an outdoor amphi-theatre, or an airport?*
- *Is the future of YTH ministry online? (Or a combination of one of these above and online?)*
- *If YTH ministry offered multiple YTH services each week to give busy teenagers a choice of attendance, would that solve the attendance issue? How could you adjust the YTH ministry to make this change at the venue, leadership, content, promotional level?*
- *Does the growing number of YTH and teenagers require the church to take Next Gen ministry more seriously? Or are we placing enough emphasis on YTH ministry now?*
- *Could it be that the main weekend church services must become produced with the teenager in mind? Would that draw families back to the faith? Is it best that the rest of the stages of the church meet in small groups throughout the week?*
- *Could the tension between the gay community and the homosexual community and politics (such as the Log Cabin endorsement of President Trump) bring another sexual revolution?*
- *Could the recent mass shootings in America bring about a different result than 9/11? How can you as a local YTH ministry work to influence safety and peace on campus?*
- *How does the social media phenomenon worsen or better our societal relationship and bring about a religious Awakening?*
- *Will the Opioid crisis change the way we handle drug dealers and teenage counseling?*

- *How can we assure that another racial incident sparks a wave of healing and unity among the people and a resurgence in church attendance, rather than anger in the media and the streets?*
- *Does another moment like the Covington Catholic teens clash in Washington teach us to not rush to judgment too quickly in a social media age? What was your initial response? And how did your response change in the weeks after?*
- *Is there more legislation in the heart of Washington like the Reproductive Health Act that will further lessen the value of life? How can YTH ministry promote healthy legislative reform?*
- *How will the obvious outrage in Washington effect bullying in the long-term future?*

"The principles of one generation will become the practices of the next generation."
-Jeff Grenell

Chapter 8

Psalm 78
The Generations Chapter: A Commentary on Psalm 78

This is the Message version (MSG) of Psalm 78. As you read this iconic psalm, you will recognize the language and the historic phrases. Some of the most notable verses in the scriptures. It is Asaph, David's writer, who pens this great Psalm. But who was Asaph? I think it is very important to know.

Asaph was in his late teens when he began writing these hymns for David. He actually became a Priest and was the chief musician and friend of David. Asaph wrote probably 12-14 of the Psalms by himself. He actually wrote more of the Bible than many other writers if you think about it. Including Jonah, Amos, Micah, Joel, Malachi, Zephaniah, Habakkuk, Nahum, Haggai, Obadiah, Peter, James, and Jude. He was there to see it all from David's leadership – the highs and the lows. But he never wavered in his love and support of David through it all.

The 78th Psalm is about the history of Israel and the importance of passing on God's truth from one generation to the next. There are iconic phrases which stand alone in the scriptures that you will remember as you read them. There are warnings of the rebellious past of Israel, challenges of the present generation to lead the younger generation, and even a sizable review of the works of God among the people.

But, what is so significant throughout this chapter is the main theme of the writing. What is clear is our responsibility in one generation of passing on the faith to the next generation. In many ways, Psalm 78 is the YTH leader's job description.

This chapter idea to provide you with a commentary on Psalm 78 to close out the book came as an idea to provide you with a generational specific commentary on the writing by Asaph. To call YTH leaders to a greater discipline in our posterity and responsibility for this generation of young people.

So, after each scripture section in the chapter, I have included some personal YTH specific commentary on each section to help further understand the importance of, not only this chapter, but, YTH ministry and leadership.

1-4 "Listen, dear friends, to God's truth,
bend your ears to what I tell you.
I'm chewing on the morsel of a proverb;
I'll let you in on the sweet old truths,
Stories we heard from our fathers,
counsel we learned at our mother's knee.
We're not keeping this to ourselves,
we're passing it along to the next generation—
God's fame and fortune,
the marvelous things he has done."

In this chapter Asaph is recalling to Israel the Life and ministry of David. He is recalling the importance of one generation leaving a heritage for the next. It is a challenge for one generation to write a narrative of theology for the next generation – the introduction of God to a new generation.

It is also a reminder of the importance of the law. Throughout the Psalms the law is called many different things. Commandments, precepts, truth, testimonies, parables, words, covenant, judgment, and statutes, are all different terms for the law. What is very clear in Psalms 78 is the importance of the history of God that is kept in the law. We find our theology – the study of God - from reading the letter of God.

We cannot lose the touch of parenting and the skin to skin and face to face relationship between parents and children. From the speaking and singing of the Word in the womb, to the nursery, to the bedroom, to the table, and to the grave. To lose this passing of the scriptures from parents to the children is to lose our way.
The principles of one generation will become the practices of the next generation and that all begins for Christians with passing the Words of God onto the next generation of children. If we fail to define God to the next generation that spells doom for any society.

Theology is the greatest story ever told and parents and YTH leaders must make sure it doesn't become the greatest story never told.

5-8

He planted a witness in Jacob,
set his Word firmly in Israel,
Then commanded our parents
to teach it to their children
So the next generation would know,
and all the generations to come—
Know the truth and tell the stories
so their children can trust in God,
Never forget the works of God
but keep his commands to the letter.
Heaven forbid they should be like their parents,
bullheaded and bad,
A fickle and faithless bunch
who never stayed true to God.

The history of the Word is set into the history of Israel and it must become the history of our modern society. Of America. And Europe. And Africa. And Asia. And of the global community. The responsibility is a commandment and not a suggestion that one generation is to prepare the next generation with this knowledge. It is a responsibility to live, tell, teach, and demonstrate theology.

But what has happened is that we have forgotten the law and we are raising a generation who are growing up and do not know theology or the important stories of scripture. They couldn't name key figures from the Bible. It is very clear that the responsibility is on the parents and YTH leaders in every generation.

What we are supposed to tell them is to never forget the activity of God, by His Spirit, in the world. How will they know the activity of God if they do not hear it from the previous generation? Because what really could happen is that the latest generation will get theology from culture and not scripture. They will get their concept of God from people who do not know God and they will end up with ideology.

The statistics in Gen Z are a result of what happens when a generation of parents and YTH leaders do not leave theology to their children. These statistics are born out of one generation who never had the Word in them to give to the generation to follow.

The Ephraimites, armed to the teeth,
ran off when the battle began.
They were cowards to God's Covenant,
refused to walk by his Word.
They forgot what he had done—
marvels he'd done right before their eyes.
He performed miracles in plain sight of their parents
in Egypt, out on the fields of Zoan.
He split the Sea and they walked right through it;
he piled the waters to the right and the left.
He led them by day with a cloud,
led them all the night long with a fiery torch.
He split rocks in the wilderness,
gave them all they could drink from underground springs;
He made creeks flow out from sheer rock,
and water pour out like a river.

When the works of God become too *familiar* to one generation, they become *foreign* to the next. It happens. Over the course of time we forget. We become familiar and calloused to the principles we were raised in. If we would simply take the time and look around us we would see God is moving and is alive and well if we are willing to see Him. But our familiarity ends up sedating us.

Asaph recounts all of the incredible things God has done for Israel. We could write a whole book on the activity of God in our lives. We could create a list just like Asaph did. A list of all of the things God has done for us to prove to our children that God is real. It would be no smaller than the list of Asaph. Yet even the remembrance of these things does not stir us to be committed. Rather, we harden our heart.

I think what we need to see is a generation of young people who demonstrate the works and the wonders of God in such a way that their generation and the generation to come will not be able to deny the existence and the evidence of God among them. The responsibility of the family and of YTH ministry is to do greater things than Jesus – at His command.

All they did was sin even more,
rebel in the desert against the High God.
They tried to get their own way with God,
clamored for favors, for special attention.
They whined like spoiled children,
"Why can't God give us a decent meal in this desert?
Sure, he struck the rock and the water flowed,
creeks cascaded from the rock.
But how about some fresh-baked bread?
How about a nice cut of meat?"

The sarcasm is beautiful. As Asaph jabs at the "snowflakes", we get the sense Israel has taken God for granted. That sounds exactly like America.

The way that Asaph is talking here, it's like he is telling us to simply remember God's activity and God's work among us. If we can see the works of God it would help us to take our eyes off from ourselves. Instead of being rebels we will become real. Instead of being selfish we would be servants. Instead of looking for something else we would see what is right there in front of us.

And the way Asaph reminds them of the works of God is through sarcasm. He asked them a series of questions that are humorous and obvious. Some of the questions Asaph asks are rhetorical at best, and sarcastic for sure.

21-31
When God heard that, he was furious—
his anger flared against Jacob,
he lost his temper with Israel.
It was clear they didn't believe God,
had no intention of trusting in his help.
But God helped them anyway, commanded the clouds
and gave orders that opened the gates of heaven.
He rained down showers of manna to eat,
he gave them the Bread of Heaven.
They ate the bread of the mighty angels;

he sent them all the food they could eat.
He let East Wind break loose from the skies,
gave a strong push to South Wind.
This time it was birds that rained down—
succulent birds, an abundance of birds.
He aimed them right for the center of their camp;
all round their tents there were birds.
They ate and had their fill;
he handed them everything they craved on a platter.
But their greed knew no bounds;
they stuffed their mouths with more and more.
Finally, God was fed up, his anger erupted—
he cut down their brightest and best,
he laid low Israel's finest young men.

In this section God is fed up and becomes angry with the response of Israel toward His faithfulness. However, even though they did not believe in Him, God continues to bless them with bread and sustenance so they were well fed and healthy. God even blessed them with the elements to keep them safe.

But they did not respond to His anger. They did not respond to His blessing. Instead, their greed and unfaithfulness and ingratitude only got worse. They just simply took God for granted and binged on all of the food He gave them.

We often do the same thing. Looking around us, we are blessed. When things are going well we coast. But when things are not going well we complain. If we do not get our way or if anything happens negative toward us we blame God.

But we might want to take a close look at this text. Because God's anger and wrath comes again as He begins to enact His judgment upon Israel for their disbelief and disobedience and ungratefulness. As a result, God judges their leaders and the young people because they could not see His blessings or His work.

32-37
And—can you believe it?—they kept right on sinning;

216

all those wonders and they still wouldn't believe!
So their lives dribbled off to nothing—
nothing to show for their lives but a ghost town.
When he cut them down, they came running for help;
they turned and pled for mercy.
They gave witness that God was their rock,
that High God was their redeemer,
But they didn't mean a word of it;
they lied through their teeth the whole time.
They could not have cared less about him,
wanted nothing to do with his Covenant.

After the wrath of God came upon them, they began to spiral downward as a society. Asaph describes Israel like a ghost town. Look around us in America today. It seems like the same thing has happened to us. When a society turns away from God and His love this is what happens. The result is like a ghost town and the life of a society is gone.

Soon after that they came running back to God. Back-and-forth. Inconsistent. Sounds like us doesn't it? If things are going bad then we turn to God and ask for help. But how deep is that repentance if it is only based upon our circumstances? We must become a generation who seeks after God no matter what and without condition.

As you read to the end of this section something remarkable happens. Asaph says Israel didn't mean a word of their repentance and we hear of the backslidden ways of Israel. We hear of their grumbling and complaining again. Israel turns away from His covenant and promises. The promises they should have been keeping and sharing with their children even when times get rough.

At the end of this section Israel has all the right things to say but they were not living the faith. No matter what is going on in the world around us, whether God is close or distant, we must be faithful to God and not become backsliders to God.

38-55
And God? Compassionate!
Forgave the sin! Didn't destroy!

217

Over and over he reined in his anger,
restrained his considerable wrath.
He knew what they were made of;
he knew there wasn't much to them,
How often in the desert they had spurned him,
tried his patience in those wilderness years.
Time and again they pushed him to the limit,
provoked Israel's Holy God.
How quickly they forgot what he'd done,
forgot their day of rescue from the enemy,
When he did miracles in Egypt,
wonders on the plain of Zoan.
He turned the River and its streams to blood—
not a drop of water fit to drink.
He sent flies, which ate them alive,
and frogs, which bedeviled them.
He turned their harvest over to caterpillars,
everything they had worked for to the locusts.
He flattened their grapevines with hail;
a killing frost ruined their orchards.
He pounded their cattle with hail,
let thunderbolts loose on their herds.
His anger flared,
a wild firestorm of havoc,
An advance guard of disease-carrying angels
to clear the ground, preparing the way before him.
He didn't spare those people,
he let the plague rage through their lives.
He killed all the Egyptian firstborns,
lusty infants, offspring of Ham's virility.
Then he led his people out like sheep,
took his flock safely through the wilderness.
He took good care of them; they had nothing to fear.
The Sea took care of their enemies for good.
He brought them into his holy land,

this mountain he claimed for his own.
He scattered everyone who got in their way;
he staked out an inheritance for them—
the tribes of Israel all had their own places.

In this long section of the chapter, Asaph begins to tell of how patient God was. God is very patient with us today also. In another Psalm David describes God as slow to anger, abounding in love and kindness, and forgiving.

Throughout the Psalms we are reminded of God's mercy and grace upon his people time and again. Several times in this text we are told Israel forgets about the works of God and they become conditional. This is what leads to their demise.

We are told of the plagues that were sent upon Israel because of their disobedience. Yet even through His anger we are told of His incredible love that was trying to win them back. God was willing to do anything He could to turn the people of Israel back to Him. The blessing and the food and the safety didn't work. Could it be the plagues might?

One last time we hear Asaph telling us God brought the people through the wilderness, through every obstacle, through their enemies and into the promised land. And He set them up in a perfect place for them to serve Him. And what happened?

56-64
But they kept on giving him a hard time,
rebelled against God, the High God,
refused to do anything he told them.
They were worse, if that's possible, than their parents:
traitors—crooked as a corkscrew.
Their pagan orgies provoked God's anger,
their obscene idolatries broke his heart.
When God heard their carryings-on, he was furious;
he posted a huge No over Israel.
He walked off and left Shiloh empty,
abandoned the shrine where he had met with Israel.
He let his pride and joy go to the dogs,

turned his back on the pride of his life.
He turned them loose on fields of battle;
angry, he let them fend for themselves.
Their young men went to war and never came back;
their young women waited in vain.
Their priests were massacred,
and their widows never shed a tear.

Almost unbelievably, Israel does it again. The works of God could not keep them. The acts of God could not win them. The goodness of God could not convince them. And the plagues had no effect upon them. It is the condition of man. That if we cannot win the battle of the spirit and the flesh then we will live at enmity between us and God

The downward spiral in this section of scripture details the foolishness of Israel to once again walk away from God no matter what He did for them.

65-72
Suddenly the Lord was up on his feet
like someone roused from deep sleep,
shouting like a drunken warrior.
He hit his enemies hard, sent them running,
yelping, not daring to look back.
He disqualified Joseph as leader,
told Ephraim he didn't have what it takes,
And chose the Tribe of Judah instead,
Mount Zion, which he loves so much.
He built his sanctuary there, resplendent,
solid and lasting as the earth itself.
Then he chose David, his servant,
handpicked him from his work in the sheep pens.
One day he was caring for the ewes and their lambs,
the next day God had him shepherding Jacob,
his people Israel, his prize possession.
His good heart made him a good shepherd;
he guided the people wisely and well.

In this last discourse Asaph defines God's love for Israel in an extraordinary way. Removing other leaders for various reasons, God appoints a new leader over them. The young boy who was appointed over them would be David.

Remarkably, demonstratively, David showed Israel how to serve Jehovah. Time and again David did mighty deeds that convinced Israel to serve Jehovah. And the result was miraculous – a comeback for Israel. Led by a teenager.

God proves to Israel how much He loved them by giving them a young example who would shepherd them and not just be their king.

At the end of the chapter, as Asaph talks about David, he chronicles how well David would lead Israel. David did not just lead with the skillfulness of his hands. He led with the integrity of his heart. God chose a man who had proven himself faithful with the sheep – his hands and his natural leadership. God chose a man who had proven himself faithful to the people – his heart and his spiritual leadership.

David was very good at what he did. David becomes God's sign to Israel of how much God loved them. What is so spectacular is that David demonstrated thousands of works for his generation. And because of these works, David left a legacy for the children to follow. Something worth telling the generations to come.

Glossary of Terms

Adolescent – The process of becoming an adult; period of time between child and adulthood

Awakening – A spiritual moment that becomes pandemic affecting large numbers of people

Code Writers – People who create or communicate behavior within a certain culture/society

Digital referee – A monitor of online connections to keep students motivated properly

Diversity valuation – Valuing diverse racial differences at the practical level of relationship

Ecology – Study of individuals and things and their relation within a context or surrounding

Epistemology – Combined learning and experiential knowledge listed in a self letter of

Gender identity – The defining of a person's identity by their gender

Gender fluidity – The changing of a person's gender by many definitions and at various times

Gen Z – The generational set born from circa 1998-2013

Gracism – The positive extension of favor and inclusion between the races

Juvenialization – Retention by adults of the traits from a previous generation or set

Microaggressions – Unconscious hidden expressions people have about race or prejudice

Millennials – The generational set born from circa 1980-1998

Missiology – Study of mission, forms, methods, and the purpose of why we do something

Moderation of Re-invention – Being careful not to lose the initial ingredients of success

Neutral site Events – Doing YTH ministry in the context of teenagers and not the church

Place-sharing – Reaching into another's context and having true empathy with them

Pop-Ups – Doing YTH ministry in spontaneous social platforms and strategic neutral sites

Publishers – The desire of teenagers to be heard through their social media and talents

Static success – It is the fact that some things will never require change at its concept level

Sustainability – The ability to maintain at a certain level or rate without depletion

The Tipping Point – When the work preceding a moment becomes a catalyst for the moment

The Teen Decade – The 7 'teen' years that only happen once in a century from (2013-2019)

YTH ministry in the Wild – Taking YTH ministry to a cultural or neutral site

Works Cited

Preface

1 https://www.un.org/YTHenvoy/wp-content/uploads/2018/09/18-00080_UN-YTH-

Strategy_Web.pdf

Chapter 1 | A History of YTH ministry: The First 100 years

1 *The Cost of Discipleship*, Bonhoeffer, Dietrich, Simon and Schuster, 1963. ISBN:

0684815001

2 *The Big Little School—200 Years of the Sunday School*, Robert L. Lynn and Elliott Wright

Abingdon Press, Abingdon Press, Nashville, TN. 1971. ISBN: B000PECIH4

3 https://ministry-to-children.com/history-of-sunday-school/

4 *High Expectations*, Rainer, Thom, B&H Books, Nashville, TN. 1999. ISBN 0805412662

5 *English Education and the Radicals 1780-1850* Harold Silver, Broadway House, London,

England, 1975. ISBN 0 7100 8212 6

6 *English Education and the Radicals 1780-1850* Harold Silver, Broadway House, London,

England, 1975. ISBN 0 7100 8212 6

7 *When God Shows Up*, Senter, Mark, Baker Book House, Grand Rapids, MI, 2010. ISBN

2009047802

8 https://www.christianitytoday.com/history/2009/august/mobilizing-generation-for-

missions.html

9 http://luke18project.com/blog/731/student-volunteer-movement-part-1/

10 http://luke18project.com/blog/731/student-volunteer-movement-part-1/

11 https://danreiland.com/?s=volunteers&submit=Search

Chapter 2 | A History of YTH ministry: The Last 100 years

1 https://billygraham.org/story/the-day-billy-graham-found-christ/

2 *Revolution*, Barna George, Tyndale House, Carol Stream, IL 2005. ISBN: 1413410161

3 *Barna Trends 2018*, Barna Research Group, Baker Book house, Grand Rapids, MI, 2018.

ISBN 9780801018640

4 *Religion and Popular Culture in America*, Bruce David Forbes, Jeffrey H. Mahan, University

of California Press, USA, 2005

5 *The Jesus Revolution*, Content, Time Magazine Cover, Volume 97, No. 25, June 21, 1971.

6 *The Jesus Movement*, Edward Plowman, David C. Cook, Elgin, IL 1971. LOC 75-147214

7 *How Billy Graham Inspired Megachurches Are Taking Over The World*, Rick Noack,

Washington Post, February 21, 2018.

8 *What to Know About Engel V. Vitale and School Prayer*, thoughtco.com/engel-v-vitale-

1962, Cline, Austin, 2019

9 https://youthworkhacks.com/a-readers-digest-history-of-youth-

ministry/?fbclid=IwAR3STZZCKKnMb4D6xSo4Akthlo9o3FMML2-

LgTUINjLTAoOA_CE0I5Egw_Y

10 https://youthworkhacks.com/a-readers-digest-history-of-youth-

ministry/?fbclid=IwAR3STZZCKKnMb4D6xSo4Akthlo9o3FMML2-

LgTUINjLTAoOA_CEOI5Egw_Y

Chapter 3 | A Theology of YTH Ministry

1 *The Cost of Discipleship*, Bonhoeffer, Dietrich, Simon and Schuster, 1963. ISBN:

0684815001

2 https://www.christianheadlines.com/columnists/al-mohler/the-pastor-as-theologian-part-

one-1390832.html

3 https://www.merriam-webster.com/dictionary/pastoral%20theology

4 https://www.christianitytoday.com/ct/2018/october/francis-chan-letters-Church-book-

acts-hyperbole.html

5 https://www.Biblehub.com/greek/2316.htm

6 https://en.oxforddictionaries.com/definition/pastoral_theology

7 https://www.newadvent.org/cathen/14611a.htm

8 https://au.thegospelcoalition.org/article/pastoral-care/

9 *Gen Z: The Culture, Beliefs, and Motivations Shaping the Next Generation*, Barna Research

Group, Ventura, CA. 2018. ISBN 9781945269134

10 *A critical Approach to Youth Culture*, Erwin, Pamela, Zondervan, Grand Rapids, MI. ISBN:

9780310292944

Chapter 4|Trends

1 *Barna Trends 2018*, Barna Research, Baker Book House, Grand Rapids, MI. 2018 ISBN

2 *Barna Trends 2018*, Barna Research, Baker Book House, Grand Rapids, MI. 2018 ISBN

3 *Gracism*: *The Art of Inclusion*, David A. Anderson, ReadHowYouWant.com Books, 2009

ISBN 9781442991705

4 *Gen Z: The Culture, Beliefs, and Motivations Shaping the Next Generation*, Barna Research

Group, Ventura, CA. 2018. ISBN 9781945269134

5 *Tell Me Who You Are*, Winona Guo and Priya Vulch, Tarcher Perigee 2019. ISBN-10:

0525541128

Chapter 5 | The Teen Decade: Interruptions

1 *The Tipping Point,* Malcolm Gladwell, Little Brown, 2000. ISBN ISBN 0-316-31696-2

2 *A Paper Boy's Fable*, Deep Patel, Post Hill Press, New York, New York, 2016. ISBN

1682610047

3 https://www1.cbn.com/churchandministry/the-roots-of-azusa-pentecost-in-topeka

4 *The Teenage Brain*, A Neuroscientist's Survival Guide to Raising Adolescents and Young

Adults, Frances E. Jensen, Amy Ellis Nutt. Harper Collins Publishers, 2015.

5 *Roots: Building the Power of Communities of Color to Challenge Structural Racism*. Akonadi

Foundation, 2010. (Definition from the Movement Strategy Center.)

Chapter 6 | How YTH Ministry Could Fail the Church

1 https://nywc.youthspecialties.com/speakers/jeanne-mayo/

2 *A Critical Approach to Youth Culture*, Pamela Erwin, Zondervan Publishing, Grand Rapids, MI 2010. ISBN 9780310292944

3 *Meet Generation Z*, White, James Emory, Baker Book House, Grand Raodis, MI 2017. ASIN B01LWY2QH2

4 *Modern Witchcraft*, https://www.glamourmagazine.co.uk/article/modern-witchcraft

5 *Faith for Exiles*, David Kinnaman, Baker Book House, Grand Rapids, MI 2019. ISBN: 0801094186

Chapter 7 | The Future of YTH Ministry

1 https://www.pewresearch.org/fact-tank/2019/02/26/the-concerns-and-challenges-of-being-a-u-s-teen-what-the-data-show/

2 *Gen Z: The Culture, Beliefs, and Motivations Shaping the Next Generation*, Barna Research Group, Ventura, CA. 2018. ISBN 9781945269134

3 *Gen Z: The Culture, Beliefs, and Motivations Shaping the Next Generation*, Barna Research Group, Ventura, CA. 2018. ISBN 9781945269134

4 *Guide to Generation Z for Marketers* A, Lynn Browne, Martech Series, 2019.

5 https://www.cfr.org/backgrounder/christianity-china

Prophetic Characteristics of The Third (Next) Great Awakening:

As I wrote this book over the last decade, these are the prophetic traits the Spirit has spoken to me that will precede *The Third (Next) Great Awakening* over the next ten years:

1. It will begin in 2020 as the Holy Spirit interrupts teenagers in various places – not only the church – camps, conventions, and seminar schedules will be placed aside
2. Church services will become interrupted with a breakout of weeping and brokenness in the pulpit and the people that will turn into weeks of laying aside the planned series and agendas of churches
3. Students will become broken for their sin and will not contain their emotions when they are praying because the Holy Spirit will burden them for their sin
4. Students will weep in all kinds of settings as they worship and confess their sin to God randomly – home, school, practice, work, and their car
5. Homes will be interrupted with a spiritual hush or pause as teenagers tell their parents of what God is doing in their life
6. When this repentance is met in the teenagers of the church (who have all of the knowledge but little action) they will see a quick discipleship process that finds them taking their faith seriously and acting upon it immediately
7. Teenagers outside of the church will see their peers lit for God and follow them into this setting and be overcome with grace and display remarkable conversions that will shock their parents when they tell them what happened to them
8. These students coming into the church will have a huge impact upon the leftover nominal church kids and cause them to commit their lives to Christ as they have never done
9. Bible reading and Christian literature will see online orders that are viral
10. The impact of this movement will result in public prayer meetings in homes, neighborhoods, communities, online, and through social apps
11. I see students in Washington on the steps of Congress and the White House in 2024 praying for America
12. Students will use their social media to preach the gospel with incredible speed and clarity and lead their friends to Christ online and through DM's
13. There will be a gaming revival in 2025 that is undeniable as miracles will break out because of prayer being offered over chat rooms and gaming boards

14. Public prayer meetings will be marked by longevity in prayer, worship, and sharing in places like board rooms, lunch rooms, cafeterias, coffee shops/restaurants, and at the end of sporting events as athletes linger on the field and in the locker-rooms praying together (people will come from the stands and join them)
15. Miracles will break out in key unchurched people in 2023 that will result in thousands being born again
16. Icons in Entertainment will continue to be born again because of the genuineness of the few who will commit to Christ first (there will be stories of Icons who are so broken and turn to Christ they cannot even publicly tell the story because of their brokenness)
17. After a very public tragic event, our government will be interrupted with brokenness and contrition and publicly apologize for their sin resulting in unprecedented unity and blessing for our nation and the resulting elected President will enjoy non-partisan support
18. The church will be overrun with so many converts that additional building and added services will need to take place to contain the growth
19. YTH ministries will be adding multiple opportunities for YTH programs in public settings to disciple students outside of the church setting – the school, coffee shops, donut shops, parks, and other venues

Made in the USA
Columbia, SC
14 January 2020